★ ★ ★ ★ ★ ★ ★ ★

How to Win a Fight with a Liberal

by Daniel Kurtzman

SOURCEBOOKS, INC.
NAPERVILLE, ILLINOIS

Published by Sourcebooks, Inc.
P.O. Box 4410, Naperville, Illinois 60567-4410
(630) 961-3900
Fax: (630) 961-2168
www.sourcebooks.com

ISBN-13: 978-1-4022-0879-9
ISBN-10: 1-4022-0879-0

Printed and bound in Canada
WC 10 9 8 7 6 5 4 3 2 1

Dedication

FOR MY WIFE,
LAURA,
AND
FOR MY PARENTS,
KEN AND CARYL,
AND MY BROTHER, TODD

Table of Contents

Introduction

Have you ever been so infuriated by a political argument that you've seriously considered reporting your opponent to Homeland Security as an enemy combatant?

Do you ever engage in heated debates with insufferable liberal moonbats, only to find yourself sputtering and stuttering, unable to articulate your beliefs?

How many times have you listened to the delusional rantings of an obnoxious colleague, loudmouthed uncle, or neighborhood blowhard while fantasizing about delivering the verbal smackdown they so richly deserve?

We've all been there—butting heads with some half-wit who refuses to submit to the inevitable wisdom of our political views. Whether you're a conservative, Republican, libertarian, independent, or someone who's just tired of liberals and their bullshit, chances are that at some point you've walked away (perhaps under the supervision of men in white coats) from a political argument seething with rage, indignation, frustration, or resentment.

Such is the sorry state of political discourse in 21st-century America. For too long, partisan Americans have had to settle for antiquated and inefficient methods of resolving their differences (incoherent rage, *Hardball* appearances, pistol duels). But it doesn't have to be this way. With a shrewd and sensible approach, you can learn to make political arguments that actually work. This book offers a roadmap to success that will help you size up, knock down, and win over your liberal rivals—without making yourself the target of an ACLU lawsuit, MoveOn.org fatwa, or Michael Moore documentary hit piece.

With the help of some basic, common-sense rules of engagement, we'll provide you with a solid foundation from which to launch your campaigns of political reeducation. We will show you how to:

★ Understand what drives your adversaries and their nutty ideas

★ Avoid deadly pitfalls that would otherwise sink your own best arguments

★ Learn how to win friends while antagonizing people

★ Identify bullshitters in their various guises

★ Slice through Swiss-cheese logic and expose fallacious reasoning

★ Make kick-ass arguments on a range of hot-button issues

★ Bludgeon your enemy with devastating sound bites, witty rejoinders, and damning facts

★ Hurl imaginative insults by selecting from 27,000 possibilities, should all else fail.

No matter what predicament you may find yourself in, this book contains indispensable tips and strategies to match your motivations. If you're hoping to rally potential recruits to a political cause, save a loved one's soul, or impress a girl, we'll show you how to maximize your chances for success. If you're looking to humiliate a pompous windbag, expose a shameless liar, or deflect an insurgent attack, we'll show you how to respond with overwhelming force.

Will you be able to win over every misguided left-wing hack? Let's be honest. Some liberals are so unteachably ignorant, so self-righteously closed-minded, there is literally nothing you can say—or no legal torture method you can employ—to enlighten them. If you're planning to mix it up with liberals who fit that profile, you'll need a blunter instrument than this book with which to beat them over the head.

Fortunately, there are plenty of liberals out there who are rational people, have a passing acquaintance with fact-based reasoning, or, failing that, are at least taking the right medication to control their condition. By following the strategies outlined here, you stand every chance of beating these types of liberals in a war of words. Or even if you can't beat them, you can jackhammer a few winning points into their brains that will send them into a tizzy of cognitive dissonance and wreak havoc on their reality.

Politics was never meant to be a spectator sport. Political debate is simply too important to be left to the so-called experts in Washington and the media who invariably just screw it up for the rest of us. That's why it falls on ordinary citizens like you—whether you're an unpracticed neophyte or a battle-scarred politico—to take matters into your own hands. If liberalism is to be defeated, the battle must be fought hand-to-hand and street-to-street. It must be fought wherever the enemy lurks—whether in the next cubicle, across the Thanksgiving dinner table, or at peace vigils, college lectures, or Dixie Chicks concerts.

It's up to you, gentle reader, to take the fight to liberals and defend America against every elitist, pagan, values-perverting, Hollywood-humping, America-blaming, terrorist-coddling ideal for which they stand.

If you don't, the moonbats will have won.

★ **CHAPTER 1** ★

What It Means to Be a Conservative

I never use the words Democrats and Republicans. It's Liberals and Americans.

—James Watt, Interior Secretary
under Ronald Reagan

There's a reason that twice as many Americans identify themselves as "conservative" as call themselves "liberal." Would you rather associate yourself with an ideology that is synonymous with patriotism, strength, freedom, family values, moral clarity, and kicking terrorist ass? Or would you rather align yourself with defeatism, elitism, permissive values, moral uncertainty, and pussyfooting with terrorists—or as it's more commonly known, liberalism?

It's not a shocker that many Americans have come to view the partisan divide in those terms. While liberals were busy spreading misery in the Carter years, doom and gloom during the Reagan and Bush I years, venereal diseases during the Clinton years, and bitter divisiveness during the Bush II years, conservatives were busy conquering communism, fighting terrorism, reforming government, and putting cold cash back in the hands of tax-weary Americans.

But now conservatives are facing a problem. They're coming off an election in which they got battered and beaten like, well, liberals. But it wasn't because voters rejected conservatism and certainly not because they endorsed liberalism (whose ranks are drying up faster than Barbara Streisand's career). Conservatives got hosed because they forgot who they are and what they stand for, and as a result lost their ability to be persuasive.

That's why, as a first step in girding for battle with liberals, it's essential to have a firm fix on your own beliefs. Take the following quiz to determine where you fit in the larger conservative mix.

 What Breed of Conservative Are You?

Choose the answers that most closely match your ideological leanings.

---

1. Which bumper sticker would you most likely put on your car?

_____A. In Case of Rapture, This Car Will Be Unmanned

_____B. If You're Gonna Burn Our Flag, Wrap Yourself in It First

_____C. Work Harder, Millions on Welfare Depend on You

_____D. Another Former Fetus for Life

_____E. Ted Kennedy's Car Has Killed More People than My Gun

_____F. No Oil for Pacifists

2. If the Founding Fathers were alive today, they would be most appalled by which of the following?

____A. The fact that you can teach our kids about condoms and clean needles but Jesus is taboo

____B. The fact that more antiwar protesters haven't been thrown in Gitmo

____C. The nation's criminally high levels of taxation

____D. The hijacking of our culture by Hollywood perverts

____E. Big government run amok

____F. The Blame America First crowd that's pampering terrorists

3. An asteroid is headed for Earth. You have a seat on the last shuttle off the planet. If you could bring only one book with which to build a future civilization, what would it be?

____A. *The Purpose-Driven Life,* by Rick Warren

____B. *The Way Things Ought to Be,* by Rush Limbaugh

____C. *The Wealth of Nations,* by Adam Smith

____D. *Culture Warrior,* by Bill O'Reilly

____E. *The NRA Guide to Firearms Assembly*

____F. *The Art of War,* by Sun Tzu

4. A second civil war has just broken out in America. Who is to blame?

_____A. Hell-bound heathens—for trying to ban God and for provoking his wrath

_____B. The liberal media—for outsourcing their foreign news coverage to Al Jazeera

_____C. Tax-and-spend socialists—for requiring every taxpayer to personally adopt a welfare queen

_____D. Activist judges—for redefining marriage as being between any person, place, or thing

_____E. Big government liberals—for trying to regulate everyone to death

_____F. Liberal freedom-haters—for helping the terrorists win

5. If you could time-travel back to any historical event and bring one thing with you, what would you choose?

_____A. The Immaculate Conception—with a video camera

_____B. September 10, 2001—with a copy of the 9/11 Commission Report

_____C. The beginning of the 1990s bull market—
with today's stock quotes

_____D. The 2004 Janet Jackson Super Bowl Halftime
Show—with a roll of duct tape

_____E. The first lunar landing—with a Confederate
flag

_____F. The end of the 1991 Gulf War—with a bunker-
busting nuke with Saddam's name on it

6. If you were a candidate for political office, what
would your theme song be?

_____A. "Onward, Christian Soldiers"

_____B. "Courtesy of the Red, White, and Blue (The
Angry American)," by Toby Keith

_____C. "Money for Nothing," by Dire Straits

_____D. "Let the Eagle Soar," by John Ashcroft

_____E. The theme song from _Law & Order_

_____F. "The Imperial March," from _Star Wars_

7. If you could pile any three people into a naked
pyramid, who would you choose?

_____A. Bill Clinton, Hillary Clinton, and Monica
Lewinsky

_____B. The Dixie Chicks

_____C. The heads of the AFL-CIO, Sierra Club, and Association of Trial Lawyers

_____D. Snoop Dog, Marilyn Manson, and Ludacris

_____E. Ted Kennedy, Nancy Pelosi, and Howard Dean

_____F. Kim Jong-il, Mahmoud Ahmadinejad, and Michael Moore

SCORING

If you answered mostly As, you're a _Faith-Based Fighter_, also known as a religious conservative. You believe in restoring God's rightful place in the public square and in politics that reflect Judeo-Christian values.

If you answered mostly Bs, you're a _Flag-Waving Everyman_, also known as a patriot. You believe in freedom, apple pie, and that God gave us a two-day weekend so we could enjoy football _and_ NASCAR.

If you answered mostly Cs, you're a _Free Marketeer_, also known as a fiscal conservative. You believe in free-market capitalism, tax cuts, and protecting your hard-earned cash from pickpocketing liberal socialists.

If you answered mostly Ds, you're a *Values Guardian*, also known as a social conservative. You believe in serving on the front lines of the culture wars to restore traditional values.

If you answered mostly Es, you're an *Antigovernment Gunslinger*, also known as a libertarian conservative. You believe in smaller government, states' rights, gun rights, and that, as Reagan once said, "The nine most terrifying words in the English language are, 'I'm from the government and I'm here to help.'"

If you answered mostly Fs, you're a *Freedom Crusader*, also known as a neoconservative. You believe in taking the fight directly to the enemy, whether it's terrorists abroad or terrorist appeasers at home.

If your answers don't match any of the above, that means you're a label-defying iconoclast or a hybrid of various types. Consider it a point of pride.

If you don't stand for anything, you don't stand for anything!

—George W. Bush

As you can see, conservatives are a diverse breed. But at bottom, there is a core set of beliefs and a common cause that unites them all. With that in mind, we present . . .

THE CONSERVATIVE MANIFESTO

Conservatives believe in an honest day's work, family values, free enterprise, keeping what you earn, and killing them before they kill us.

Conservatives believe in NASCAR, neighborhood barbecues, Sunday sermons, the Ten Commandments, fair and balanced news, faithfully interpreting the Constitution, and that America would be a safer place if Clinton had spent his eight years in office protecting America rather than fiddling with cigars and porking chubby girls.

Conservatives believe in a shining city on a hill, and in protecting that shining city from terrorists, illegal aliens, and social welfare parasites.

Conservatives believe that there ought to be a constitutional amendment requiring that every liberal who threatens to move to Canada actually has to move to Canada.

Conservatives believe if there is such a thing as global warming and if rising oceans flood the planet, you're going to need a bad-ass SUV to get around.

Conservatives believe any short list for secretary of defense should include Jack Bauer, Chuck Norris, and Arnold Schwarzenegger.

Conservatives believe in moments of silence, border security, terrorist surveillance, preemptive war, the power of the markets, states' rights, the right to life, liberating people so they may live in freedom, and that listening to Hollywood liberals talk about values is like listening to the French talk about military deterrence.

And above all, conservatives have unwavering faith in the strength and character of the American people and every confidence that our great nation will triumph in the struggle over the twin evils of our time—terrorism and liberalism.

Rate Your Partisan Intensity Quotient (PIQ)

Beyond basic ideology, we also need to assess your partisan temperament. Are you the type of person who eagerly engages liberals in debate, or do you avoid confrontation at all costs? Answer the following questions, and we'll rate your PIQ.

1. Your neighbor has just placed a very large Hillary 2008 sign on her lawn. Do you:

_____A. Respect her right to free speech?

_____B. Put up an even larger Giuliani 2008 sign?

_____C. Take down her sign in the middle of the night?

_____D. Graffiti your own Giuliani sign and then publicly accuse her of defacing your property?

2. You're at a Republican campaign rally when you encounter a smelly hippie with multiple body piercings hoisting a sign that that says "Jesus Save Us—from the Republicans." Do you:

_____A. Embrace him in the spirit of brotherly love?

_____B. Move to another part of the crowd to avoid a confrontation?

_____C. Hoist up your own sign to block him from the cameras and the podium?

_____D. Wrestle him to the ground and smack him repeatedly with your Bible?

3. You're stuck in a traffic jam created by antiwar protesters blocking an intersection. Do you:

_____A. Sit in your car patiently while the police clear the street?

_____B. Blast Rush Limbaugh on the radio to drown out their chanting?

_____C. Honk and shout epithets?

_____D. Try to get through to NORAD to call in air strikes?

4. You've just been given the opportunity to meet Hillary Clinton and have a brief face-to-face encounter. Would you:

_____A. Tell her what an honor it is to meet her?

_____B. Think about what a horrid wench she is but hold your tongue out of respect?

_____C. Grill her on her plan for victory in Iraq?

_____D. Ask her how anyone can expect to believe she's smart enough to run the country, when she wasn't smart enough to figure out her husband was cheating on her?

SCORING YOUR PIQ

Award yourself zero points for every A, one point for every B, two points for every C, and three points for every D.

11–12: Severe ★★★★★★★★★★★★

You're a *Flame-Throwing Revolutionary*. You may be one restraining-order violation away from jail.

8–10: High ★★★★★★★★★★

You're a *Fierce Fighter*. You will argue politics any time and any place, even when it's not the topic at hand.

5–7: Elevated ★★★★★★★

You're a *Passionate Foot Soldier*. You readily engage in political debate but are apt to bail out before things get too testy.

2–4: Guarded ★★★★

You're a *Polite Observer*. You partake in the occasional political discussion, but generally get more satisfaction over arguing about *American Idol* than you do arguing politics.

0–1: Low ★

You're a *Noncombatant*. You're liable to wave the white flag and run for the hills at the slightest sign of political discord. Time to grow a pair.

WHAT'S YOUR STATE OF EMBATTLEMENT?

Everyone is familiar with the much-ballyhooed red vs. blue divide, which neatly separates America into Republican and Democratic states. But that obviously doesn't tell the whole story, because no state is uniformly red or blue. You've heard of other regional divides like the Bible Belt and the Rust Belt, but there are many other "belts" that describe partisan America. To determine your State of Embattlement, locate the belt below that most closely corresponds to your specific locality.

THE BELTS OF BLUE AMERICA

If you are a conservative living in . . .

The Brokeback Belt (gay havens across America)

The Bagel Belt (urban areas with a high concentration of wisecracking Jews)

The Botox Belt (the land of the rich and plastic, from Manhattan to Hollywood)

The Ivory Tower Belt (enclaves dominated by intellectual and academic elites)

The Tofurky Belt (the land of militant vegans and naked tree-huggers)

The Bong Belt (stoner country, e.g., the core demographic of *The Daily Show* and *Real Time with Bill Maher*)

. . .you are *Desperately Besieged*. You're surrounded by so many liberals, it's like being the last person left at the end of a zombie movie. Arguing with them seems like a lost cause, and the best you can do is lay low and hide, lest they suck out your brain and turn you into one of them.

THE BELTS OF PURPLE AMERICA

If you are a conservative living in . . .

The Slot Jockey Belt (casino country, e.g., Nevada, Atlantic City, the Mississippi River Valley)

The Stroke Belt (retirement communities in Florida)

The Kitsch Belt (small towns built around roadside kitsch and tourist schlock)

The Can't-Buckle-My Belt (where the hefty portions match the people)

The Cookie-Cutter Belt (middle-class, planned communities resembling *Desperate Housewives*'s Wisteria Lane)

The Bud Belt (where canned, flavor-free beer will always be king)

. . . you are *Battle-Hardened*. You have so many fights you want to pick with the liberals all around you that you may not even know where to start.

THE BELTS OF RED AMERICA

If you are a conservative living in . . .

The Chastity Belt (southern and middle America, where abstinence is all the rage)

The Saved Belt (God-fearing, churchgoing middle America)

The Dow Jones Belt (financial centers from New York to Chicago to Houston)

The Locked and Loaded Belt (gun country)

The Caviar and Cocaine Belt (home to the old money, country-club set)

The Border Belt (where 700-mile fences magically secure 2,000-mile borders)

. . .you are *Safely Entrenched*. You're surrounded by so many people who agree with you that your arguing skills may have gone flabby from disuse.

Whatever situation you find yourself in, your goal is the same: Engage your enemies wherever they lurk. But first you must understand your enemy. . .

★ CHAPTER 2 ★

Know Your Enemy

If you know the enemy and know yourself, you need not fear the result of a hundred battles. If you know yourself but not the enemy, for every victory gained you will also suffer a defeat.

—Sun Tzu, *The Art of War*

Before you engage liberals in combat, it's important to have a clear understanding of exactly who your enemies are, including their core beliefs, specific ideological profile, and vision for America. Doing so will enable you to better dissect, ridicule, and exploit their weaknesses for maximum advantage.

For starters, here's a look at what liberals truly stand for.

THE LIBERAL MANIFESTO

Liberals believe that singing songs, holding hands, waving candles, and holding up a sign printed with "Think Peace" can solve all the world's problems.

Liberals believe in endless tax hikes, cradle-to-grave welfare, drive-through abortions, and that playing the victim, flip-flopping, and cutting-and-running ought to be Olympic demonstration sports.

Liberals believe in *Brokeback Mountain* majesties, fruited planes of exposed nipples, and amber waves of girls gone wild.

Liberals believe in taking away your money, your guns, your crucifix, and your non-vegetable oil–fueled car.

Liberals believe in blaming America first, burning the flag, demoralizing our troops, and that there's nothing the U.S. military does that a UN-sponsored delegation of lawyers, therapists, and naked hippie demonstrators can't do better.

Liberals believe in candidates who like to feel your pain, grope your daughter, drop their trousers, and drive their dates off a bridge.

Liberals believe that if people want to marry their same-sex partner, their pet, their blow-up doll, or their cardboard cutout of Ryan Seacrest, that's their right as an American.

Liberals believe in lecturing you about the many ways in which you are oppressing them through your racism, heterosexism, classism, ageism, ableism, lookism, sizeism, heightism, and hygieneism.

Liberals believe the polar ice caps are going to melt any day now and turn the Rocky Mountains into oceanfront property.

And worst of all, liberals believe that your failure to share their belief in all of the above makes you a politically incorrect, intolerant, bigoted, uninformed, evil, stupid, fascist moron from "fly-over country."

Never underestimate the power of stupid
people in large groups.

—Anonymous

A FIELD GUIDE TO THE LIBERAL GENUS

Now it's time for you to meet the various species that make up the Democratic voting bloc. Familiarize yourself with this handy field guide so that you can quickly size up your opponent.

GRANOLACRATS

Liberal environmental activists dedicated to the proposition that all men, spotted owls, and bean sprouts are created equal

AKA: Tree-huggers, envirofreaks, ecowackos, ecoterrorists

Natural habitat: Small coastal cities, college towns, and suburbs with a suitable climate for growing cannabis

Turn-ons: Spotted owls, windmills, naked yoga, ozone, weed, vandalizing SUVs

Turn-offs: Fossil fuels, displaced caribou,

deodorant, toilet paper containing less than 50 percent recycled fibers

Likely to be seen: Forming a human chain around an Oscar Mayer Weinermobile while wearing T-shirts printed with "Pigs Are Friends—Not Food."

Would sooner be caught dead than: Wearing non-fair-trade sandals

OPPRESSEDBYTERIANS

Oppressed, left-wing agitators primarily concerned with social injustice, the suppression of minority rights, and more importantly, trying to make every friend, relative, or passerby feel guilty about it

AKA: Disadvantaged Democrats, identity politics activists, PC Police, feminazis, victims

Natural habitat: College campuses, inner cities, nonprofit organizations

Turn-ons: Political correctness, welfare, affirmative action, amnesty for illegals, gangsta rap, chocolate cities

Turn-offs: "The Man"

Likely to be seen: Berating you and recommending "sensitivity training" for using terms like "poor," "lazy," and "crackhead" rather than "economically marginalized," "motivationally challenged," and "artificial-stimulant victim"

Would sooner be caught dead than: Pledging allegiance to a non-rainbow flag

NPR PARROT-TROOPERS

Tax-applauding, big government-touting, latte-drinking elites who believe that parroting sound bites from National Public Radio constitutes an act of civil disobedience

AKA: latte liberals, limousine liberals, liberal elites, establishment liberals

Natural habitat: Wealthy urban enclaves and posh suburbs, heavily concentrated in ivory towers, beach condos, Starbucks cafés, and French restaurants

Turn-ons: Sushi, Botox, flip-flops, windsurfing, class warfare

Turn-offs: FOX News, the NRA, SUVs (except their own), bad feng shui, public displays of the Ten Commandments

Likely to be seen: Eating *foie gras* at a Harry Belafonte benefit concert for the Hillary Clinton Legal Defense Fund

Would sooner be caught dead than: In church

HOLLYWOOD IGNORATI

Politically active Hollywood liberals who believe everyone has an obligation to hear and affirm their glamorous, morally superior opinions

AKA: Celebricrats, celiberals, Hollywood elites

Natural habitat: Gated, hillside LA homes, posh Manhattan penthouses, drug recovery centers

Turn-ons: Ethiopian orphans, Versace, Kabbalah, orgies, shotgun divorces, starvation diets, drunk driving

Turn-offs: Everything else

Likely to be seen: Driving a stretch Hummer to their private jet after lecturing people about energy conservation

Would sooner be caught dead than: Accepting an award without first denouncing President Bush

MOORE-ONS

Stoned slackers and knee-jerk cynics who would believe Michael Moore was the second coming of Jesus Christ if they weren't godless heathens

AKA: MoveOn.org liberals, Daily Kos liberals, Generation X, Y, and Whatever

Natural habitat: Their parents' basements

Turn-ons: The Daily Show, conspiracy theories, Internet porn, towering bongs

Turn-offs: The Bush "criminal empire," imperialism, every major corporation with the exception of Krispy Kreme and Domino's Pizza

Likely to be seen: Threatening to move to Canada

Would sooner be caught dead than: Living in Canada

KUMBAYANIKS

Peace-loving, patchouli oil–covered hippies who believe in ridiculously oversimplified slogans, not war

AKA: Peaceniks, pacifists, Vichycrats, French cheese–eating surrender monkeys

Natural habitat: Geodesic domes, tie-dyed Volkswagen campers, Burning Man

Turn-ons: Recreating the '60s, burning flags, appeasing terrorists, smoking weed with their kids

Turn-offs: The Patriot Act, tear gas, taser guns, anyone with a "Support Our Troops" bumper sticker

Likely to be seen: Asking themselves "WWCSD?" (What Would Cindy Sheehan Do?)

Would sooner be caught dead than: Showering

OTHER LIBERAL SPECIES YOU MAY ENCOUNTER

Hillary Krishnas: Devout liberals who long to restore a Clintonian government with all of the liberal idealism and none of the fellatio

Conflagrationists: Radical, flag-burning anarchists who hurl garbage cans through Starbucks windows (*after* buying their grandé mocha frappuccinos)

Tinfoilies: Conspiracy-obsessed, tinfoil hat–wearing, paranoid freaks who believe, among other things, that the 9/11 plot was hatched by the government, Ken Lay faked his death, and aliens are being held at Area 51

ACL-eunuchs: Extremely voluble left-wing activists who can be heard whining and shrieking like impotent choir boys about disappearing civil liberties

Commiekazis: Left-wing pinko commies who rail against capitalism and believe America could achieve greatness if only it were Cuba

West Wingbats: Self-deluding liberals for whom watching reruns of *The West Wing* is reality TV

Pangaytheists: Urban professional sodomites whose rallying cry is "We're here, we're registered at Bloomingdales; get used to it."

Hell is other people.

—Jean-Paul Sartre

How to Rate a Liberal's Partisan Intensity Quotient (PIQ)

In addition to being familiar with various liberal species, you will also need to gauge the extent of your opponent's partisan passion, inflexibility, or possible pathology. You can quickly determine your opponent's PIQ with this simple test. Award one point for each "yes" answer.

_____**1.** Do they send out long, expository political emails?

_____**2.** Are the emails written in all caps, riddled with expletives, and sent to large distribution lists?

_____**3.** Do they own any CDs by Melissa Etheridge, Kanye West, or Rage Against the Machine?

_____**4.** Do they own a copy of "The Communist Manifesto," *Quotations from Chairman Mao Tse-Tung*, or anything written by Michael Moore?

_____**5.** Do they frequently quote from Al Gore's *An Inconvenient Truth* or The Weather Channel?

_____**6.** Do they go around boasting about how their carbon footprint is smaller than yours?

_____**7.** Have they ever chastised you for voting the wrong way?

_____**8.** Have they ever tried to get you to change your vote by bribing, blackmailing, shaming, or seducing you?

_____**9.** Do they frequently blame Bush for the world's problems?

_____**10.** Do they frequently blame Bush for things like inclement weather, the Yankees' losing streak, or their erectile dysfunction?

SCORING

9–10: SEVERE
Your opponent is an Unhinged Extremist.
Approach with extreme caution.

7–8: HIGH
Your opponent is a Pugnacious Pitbull.
Hit 'em with everything you've got.

4–6: ELEVATED
Your opponent is a Dedicated Disciple.
You're in for a serious scuffle.

2–3: GUARDED
Your opponent is a Casual Combatant.
Crush 'em with overwhelming force.

0–1: LOW
Your opponent is a Guaranteed Pushover.
Show no mercy.

> The liberal is continually angry, as only a self-important man can be, with his civilization, his culture, his country, and his folks back home. His is an infantile worldview. At the core of a liberal is the spoiled child—miserable, as all spoiled children are, unsatisfied, demanding, ill-disciplined, despotic, and useless. Liberalism is a philosophy of sniveling brats.
>
> —P. J. O'Rourke

FREQUENTLY ASKED QUESTIONS ABOUT LIBERALS

Now that you know whom you're dealing with, it's time to get to the vexing questions about liberals' peculiar behavior and seemingly inexplicable belief system.

Q. Why are liberals so damn angry all the time?

A. If you'd lost seven out of the last ten presidential elections, watched your party leaders spend most of their time arguing with each other, and seen your very ideology turn into such a dirty word that you were embarrassed to even admit you were a liberal, the veins in your forehead would be perpetually throbbing too. Plus, no one wears deodorant at their rallies.

Q. Why do liberals have such a hard time taking a simple stand on an issue? Why are they always for something one day, then against it the next?

A. No one really knows why, but some experts speculate that because they spend so much time holding their fingers to the wind, they don't get enough blood flow to their brains.

Q. Is there anything liberals consistently stand for?

A. To answer that, first you must pay a question tax.

Q. Do all liberals endorse sexually permissive, deviant behavior?

A. It depends on what the meaning of the word "yes" is.

Q. How can anyone expect liberal Democrats to solve the nation's problems when all they do is whine and gripe? Do they even have a plan?

A. Democrats actually have a carefully thought-out, multipronged approach to problem solving, consisting of the following steps: (1) conduct a focus group to identify a problem; (2) propose tax hikes as solution; (3) accuse anyone who opposes said solution of intolerance; (4) conduct an opinion poll to gauge support; (5) reverse position; (6) debate themselves endlessly over whether they have, in fact, reversed position; (7) deny that the problem exists; (8) do nothing while Republicans fix the problem.

Q. Liberals seem to take themselves way too seriously. Why won't they lighten up already?

A. Liberals are appalled that you would even ask that question at a time when glaciers need refreezing, wetlands need rewetting, deadbeat crackheads need handouts, underprivileged minorities need guaranteed college admittance, and illegal immigrants need citizenship. Until then, everyone else must be made to suffer.

The Democrats seem to be basically nicer people, but they have demonstrated time and again that they have the management skills of celery. They're the kind of people who'd stop to help you change a flat but would somehow manage to set your car on fire. I would be reluctant to entrust them with a Cuisinart, let alone the economy.

—Dave Barry

A GLIMPSE INTO THE LIBERAL UTOPIA

Liberals are working hard to build a society that realizes their dreams for total domination over America's political and cultural landscape. Whether they succeed or fail will depend on your commitment to derailing their plans. To illustrate what's at stake, here's a glimpse into America's possible future should liberals have their unfettered way with the country.

NEWSPAPER HEADLINES LIBERALS WOULD LOVE TO SEE

❗ Gay Marriage Legalized; Hillary Clinton, Janet Reno Wed in White House Rose Garden Ceremony

❗ President Clooney Taps Cindy Sheehan for Defense Secretary

❗ School Sex Ed Broadened to Include Alternative Lifestyles, Live Demonstrations

❗ Global Warming Solved Following Worldwide Oil Ban; Triumphant President Gore Takes Cross-Country Victory Lap in Horse Carriage One

❗ U.S. Troops Join French Military in Training Exercises, Learn to March Backward

❗ Supreme Court Legalizes Marijuana, Crack, and Heroin; Ruling Rife With Grammatical Errors, Multiple Uses of Word "Dude"

- ❗ Global Terrorist Leaders Invited to Camp David for Self-Esteem–Building Summit, Yoga Retreat
- ❗ Ninth Circuit Upholds Death Penalty for Citizens Who Refuse to Recycle
- ❗ President Dean Approves Construction of Roman-Style Coliseum on National Mall; Evangelical Christians to Be Fed to Lions as Part of New National Pastime
- ❗ Smithsonian's New Lesbian Gay Bisexual Transgender Queer Questioning Intersex (LGBTQQI) Heritage Museum Welcomes 100-Millionth Visitor

Don't think it could ever happen? Well, no one ever thought a draft-dodging, pot-smoking, intern-groping perjurer could get elected president twice, be impeached, and then make a viable bid to become first "lady." Not to put too much pressure on you, but if you don't do your part to help frustrate their plans, the liberal utopians will have won.

CHAPTER 3

Can't We All Just Get Along?

As Americans, we must ask ourselves: Are we really so different? Must we stereotype those who disagree with us? Do we truly believe that ALL red-state residents are ignorant racist fascist knuckle-dragging NASCAR-obsessed cousin-marrying roadkill-eating tobacco juice-dribbling gun-fondling religious-fanatic rednecks; or that ALL blue-state residents are godless unpatriotic pierced-nose Volvo-driving France-loving left-wing communist latte-sucking tofu-chomping holistic-wacko neurotic vegan weenie perverts?

—Dave Barry

L et's face it. Our great nation has been divided along fierce partisan lines ever since the days of our founding fathers, when even our finest, powdered wig–wearing, silk stocking–strutting statesmen exchanged bitter recriminations over who was the bigger girlie man.

With liberals and conservatives, Democrats and Republicans, and Blue Staters and Red Staters growing more polarized by the day, is there any hope left of finding common ground? The answer is yes. But before we get to that, let's first take stock of America's current state of disunion to discover exactly how deeply and ridiculously divided we have become.

A Day in the Life of Conservatives vs. Liberals

Conservatives and liberals may live in the same cities and breathe the same air, but they might as well be gliding along two separate planes of existence.

A Day in the Life of a Conservative	A Day in the Life of a Liberal
☆ **7:00 a.m.**	
Wake up, flip on FOX News, pick outfit to match terror alert level	Wake up, wash down morning-after pill with hot cup of chai tea
☆ **8:00 a.m.**	
Bible study	Pilates
☆ **8:30 a.m.**	
Listen to Rush Limbaugh while idling in the Krispy Kreme drive-through line	Read *The New York Times* while sipping a latte at Starbucks
☆ **9 a.m.**	
Arrive at work, force the community's last mom-and-pop shop out of business	Arrive at work at non-profit organization, sharpen pencil
☆ **10 a.m.**	
Buy hundred-share lot of Bechtel stock in anticipation of war with Iran	Buy flock of chicks from Heifer International to donate to Kenyan village

A Day in the Life of a Conservative	A Day in the Life of a Liberal
★ **12 p.m.**	
Eat sandwich of leftover squab from weekend hunt, washed down with Bud	Enjoy bag lunch of braised fennel, watercress, and wheat grass juice
★ **3 p.m.**	
Gas up Hummer, reposition Confederate flag on window, clean homeless person off grille	Pump air in bicycle tires, lecture passing drivers about evils of internal combustion engine
★ **5 p.m.**	
Stop by drugstore for Viagra prescription, report suspicious-looking cashier to INS for deportation	Stop by drugstore for Prozac prescription, file punitive damage lawsuit after being told it isn't ready
★ **6 p.m.**	
Join the guys at Hooters to watch ESPN and ogle the waitstaff over a couple of pitchers	Join fellow tree huggers to block commuter traffic until the city agrees to build a "toad tunnel" allowing frogs to safely cross busy street

A Day in the Life of a Conservative	A Day in the Life of a Liberal
★ 7:30 p.m.	
Sit down to family dinner, discuss Pat Robertson's latest warning about how eating soy products can make you gay	Sit down to family dinner, discuss Sean Penn's recent op-ed on global security challenges of the 21st century
★ 8 p.m.	
Watch *The O'Reilly Factor* for fair and balanced news coverage	Watch *The Daily Show* for fair and balanced news
★ 10:00 p.m.	
Have missionary-position sex with spouse	Invite the neighbors over for a group orgy
★ 11 p.m.	
Recite prayers, await the Rapture	Smoke joint, fall asleep

> The Democrats are the party of government activism, the party that says government can make you richer, smarter, taller, and get the chickweed out of your lawn. Republicans are the party that says government doesn't work, and then get elected and prove it.
>
> —P. J. O'Rourke

Battle of the Bumper Stickers

There's no better illustration of the stark partisan split than the ideological battle that conservatives and liberals are waging every day on America's roadways.

Popular Liberal Bumper Stickers

★ The Rapture Is *Not* an Exit Strategy

★ May the Fetus You Save Be Gay

★ Evolution Is Just a Theory . . . Kind of Like Gravity

★ Bush Never Exhaled

★ Nice Hummer—Sorry About Your Penis

★ The Republican Party: Our Bridge to the 11th Century

★ America: One Nation Under Surveillance

★ Would Someone Give Bush a Blowjob So We Can Impeach Him?
★ I'm Already against the *Next* War
★ That's OK, I Wasn't Using My Civil Liberties Anyway
★ Stewart / Colbert 2008
★ At Least in Vietnam Bush Had an Exit Strategy

Popular Conservative Bumper Stickers
★ Run, Hillary, Run (placed on front bumper)
★ Protest Noted. Now Shut the Hell Up!
★ Spotted Owls Taste Like Chicken
★ If Guns Kill People, then Spoons Make Michael Moore Fat
★ Vote Democrat, It's Easier than Thinking
★ In Case of Rapture, this Car Will Be Unmanned
★ My SUV Can Beat Up Your Prius
★ Stop Global Whining
★ Silly Liberal, Paychecks Are for Workers
★ If Ignorance Is Bliss, You Must Be One Happy Liberal
★ Don't Like My Flag? Call 1-800-Leave-the-USA
★ Except for Ending Slavery, Fascism, Nazism, and Communism, War Has Never Solved Anything

Conservative, n: A statesman who is enamored of existing evils, as distinguished from the Liberal, who wishes to replace them with others.

—Ambrose Bierce

What Conservatives Say vs. What Liberals Hear

Most conservatives and liberals who have spent any time in the partisan trenches quickly discover that even basic attempts at communication can be utterly futile. Thanks to ingrained stereotypes, built-in defense mechanisms, and intense partisan conditioning, a conservative may say one thing, but a liberal is almost certain to hear something else. As you can see here, it's not pretty.

What conservatives say: We need to protect the sanctity of life, defend the sanctity of marriage, and teach our children the virtues of abstinence.

What liberals hear: We need to bomb abortion clinics, ban gay people, and fit our children with chastity belts.

What conservatives say: We need to reduce our dependency on foreign oil by pursuing oil exploration at home.

What liberals hear: We're going to drill for oil in the Alaskan wilderness, Yellowstone, and if necessary, Disneyworld.

What conservatives say: We need to crack down on illegal immigration.

What liberals hear: We need to crack down on illegal immigration after the cleaning crew at Wal-Mart finishes the night shift and Jorge mows my lawn.

What conservatives say: Family values are stronger in the red states.

What liberals hear: If you ignore the higher rates of divorce, teen pregnancy, and wife beatings, family values are stronger in the red states.

What conservatives say: Liberals are all a bunch of Hollywood-loving, gun-grabbing, stem cell–sucking, abortion-promoting, Michael Moore–worshipping, trial lawyer–humping, troop-slandering, terrorist-coddling defeatocrats who are hellbent on destroying America.

What liberals hear: Sieg heil!

WHAT LIBERALS SAY VS. WHAT CONSERVATIVES HEAR

There's no better luck on the flip side:

What liberals say: I'm tired of listening to religious nutcases and puritanical prudes trying to dictate what I do in the bedroom or what I can do with my body.

What conservatives hear: I'm a godless, amoral hedonist. Where's the nearest drive-through abortion clinic?

What liberals say: The media does not have a liberal bias.

What conservatives hear: The earth is not round.

What liberals say: No war for oil.

What conservatives hear: My total comprehension of foreign policy is limited to four words.

What liberals say: We must fight for the people against the powerful.

What conservatives hear: The proletariat must rise up against the bourgeoisie, seize the means of production, and unite with the workers of the world.

What liberals say: Conservatives are all a bunch of warmongering, deficit-expanding, pollution-spewing, torture-sanctioning, civil liberty–seizing, New Orleans–abandoning, military-wrecking, Armageddon-yearning, fanatical bigots who have done more to destroy American democracy than Osama bin Laden ever dreamed.

What conservatives hear: I hate America, I hate freedom, and I hate myself.

COMMON ENEMIES WE CAN ALL AGREE TO HATE

OK, now that it's abundantly clear how hopelessly estranged and deranged the two warring sides have become, it's time to find that elusive common ground.

It's been said that what divides us as a country is not nearly as strong as what unites us. And what could unite us more than our common enemies? With that in mind, let us embark on the path to bipartisan unity by taking a moment to jointly revile some of the most odious miscreants, evil-doers, and entities that liberals and conservatives can agree to hate.

You can, of course, never go wrong bashing the likes of Al Qaeda, Osama bin Laden, Kim Jong-il, Mahmoud Ahmadinejad, corporate criminals, and pedophiles. But if you really want to bond with liberals, try trash-talking the following enemies of freedom, all of whom pose a more immediate threat to our collective sanity.

★ ★ ★ ★ ★ ★ ★ ★ ★

President Josiah Bartlet:
  We agree on nothing, Max.
Senator Max Lobell: Yes, sir.
Bartlet: Education, guns, drugs, school prayer, gays, defense spending, taxes— you name it, we disagree.
Lobell: You know why?
Bartlet: Because I'm a lily-livered, bleeding-heart, liberal, egghead communist.
Lobell: Yes, sir. And I'm a gun-toting, redneck son-of-a-bitch.
Bartlet: Yes, you are.
Lobell: We agree about that.
      —NBC's *The West Wing*

> I view America like this: 70-80 percent [are] pretty reasonable people that truthfully, if they sat down, even on contentious issues, would get along. And the other 20 percent of the country run it.
>
> —Jon Stewart

THE MEDIA

Conservatives complain that the media has a grotesque liberal bias. Liberals say the media practically gets down on its knees to service conservatives. Either way, you can count on the mainstream media to botch the facts and distort the truth in the race to get the story wrong first. Sure, there are some intrepid journalists doing important work, but as a whole, the establishment media is a brainless, sensationalistic, and unstoppable force that you can rely on to saturate the airwaves with wall-to-wall coverage of the latest missing white blonde girl, ignore the current genocidal war in Africa, blindly regurgitate partisan talking points, and, occasionally, make up stories out of whole cloth.

INTERNET SPAMMERS

There's a special molten cauldron on reserve in hell for the creators of Internet spam. These are the stalkers and perverts who sit around coming up with radically moronic message headings that clog up your inbox, such as "Buff up your boner," "Let Yoda refinance your house," "Hot deals on Iraqi real estate," and "We have located several horny women in your area!" Forget Al Qaeda. Let's go after them.

GERALDO RIVERA

The mustachioed, sensationalistic television reporter was asked to leave Iraq after giving away U.S. troop positions, bragged about carrying a gun in Afghanistan that he wasn't afraid to use, claimed to be at the scene of a friendly fire incident when he was actually 300 miles away, and reportedly made an elderly Hurricane Katrina victim shoot multiple takes of him heroically rescuing her. He has also cried repeatedly on camera, often with little provocation. You won't find a better personification of everything that is insipid, self-aggrandizing, and soulless about celebrity journalism.

THE IRS

It's bad enough that our tax code is incomprehensible to intelligent man, but what really pisses everyone off is how ineptly and inconsistently our tax laws are enforced. The IRS is more likely to pester and probe the average working stiff than the average millionaire or the corporation that's squirreling away money in a Cayman Islands tax shelter. What's worse, every time you publicly mouth off against the IRS (say, in the pages of a book that names the IRS as an enemy of the people), you're almost sure to be audited.

TOM CRUISE

When not jumping up and down on couches, convincing Katie Holmes to carry his demon spawn, angrily impugning psychiatry, or making craptacular movies, Tom Cruise can be found touting a crackpot religion known as Scientology—an elaborately disguised pyramid scam created by a second-rate science-fiction writer. It's based on the perfectly plausible belief that humans are descended from aliens who were frozen by an evil galactic overlord 75 million years ago, brought to Earth in a spaceship, dropped into volcanoes, and blown up with hydrogen bombs. Cruise is not only giving his fellow intergalactic travelers a bad name, but if he is not contained, he may continue to pose a clear and present danger to nubile Hollywood starlets throughout the universe.

★ CHAPTER 4 ★

Basic Training

The definition of insanity is doing the same
thing over and over again and expecting different results.

—Albert Einstein, attributed

There's a right way to engage liberals in combat and a wrong way. The right way will
enable you to make forceful arguments,
win hearts and minds, and be greeted as a liberator.
The wrong way will alienate your opponents, make
them harden their position, and get you kicked out
of public places.

Unfortunately, due to inadequate preparation and training—or sheer self-delusion—many people embark on the wrong path. To help you gird for battle and avert certain disaster, we'll show you in this chapter how to avoid key pitfalls, pick the right fights, and turn arguments to your advantage by following some basic rules of engagement.

THE SEVEN HABITS OF HIGHLY INEFFECTIVE PARTISANS

As with many things in life, we are often our own worst enemies. These seven habits are like kryptonite to the partisan warrior and must be painstakingly avoided.

1. BECOMING OVERLY EMOTIONAL

There's nothing more counterproductive to your cause—or costly to your metaphysical well-being—than becoming emotionally unraveled in the middle of an argument. If you're experiencing heart palpitations, developing blurred vision, or emitting cartoon steam from your nostrils while your opponent is sitting there stone-faced, you're not winning. Keep your rage in check at all times, and don't take things personally.

2. OOZING CONDESCENSION

Even if you believe you're talking to a breath-takingly misguided ignoramus, conceal it. If you patronize or belittle your opponents, they'll only dig in their heels. They'll also think that you're a sanctimonious, pompous wanker.

3. SPEWING HATEFUL INVECTIVE

There's nothing wrong with using hard-charging rhetoric and sharp-edged words, but you need to stop short of savage insults, epithets, and ridiculously inflammatory rhetoric (e.g., calling Democrats terrorist lovers or godless, baby-killing feminazis). Many media bloviators have built entire careers on hysterical diatribes, but that only works when you're preaching to the choir. Back on planet Earth, you'll never succeed in making a winning argument if you come off as a raging misanthrope.

4. TALKING WITHOUT LISTENING

You have a lot to say—everybody does—but if you aren't willing to engage in a dialogue and try to understand your opponent's viewpoint, you're not going to get anywhere. Worse, you will bore your audience to pieces. Unless you are a master hypnotist, command a pulpit, or people are actually paying money to listen to you, pipe down and yield the floor.

5. INVENTING FACTS ON THE FLY

If you don't have the facts on hand to back up your argument, don't make them up. The facts will eventually catch up with you, and you'll be exposed as the fraud that you are.

6. MAKING SWEEPING GENERALIZATIONS

Even if you believe it's true that all liberals hate America, freedom, the military, capitalism, and God, the problem with those kinds of flat declarations is that you create too much territory to defend. It also makes it much easier for your opponent to knock down your arguments. Instead, be specific, and only state what is necessary to make your case, such as that Michael Moore hates America, freedom, the military, capitalism, and God.

7. BECOMING CONSPIRATORIAL

It's tempting to believe that there are sinister liberal forces engaged in grand, diabolical schemes (e.g., the DNC is actively conspiring with Al Qaeda, Mel Gibson was framed by a Zionist cabal, and Bill Clinton is actually a latent homosexual). Don't bother going there. There are plenty of good arguments to make without bringing in the vast conspiracy of little green men on the grassy knoll. And besides, as anyone who has worked in government will tell you, the government isn't competent enough to pull off a decent conspiracy.

How Woefully Ineffective Are You?

Now let's identify whether you're predisposed to any of the seven deadly habits. Answer these questions about how you would handle yourself in the following situations.

1. You're standing around the water cooler listening to a colleague rant about the foolishness of tax cuts. She's arguing that they don't help the economy and only make the rich richer. Do you:

_____A. Laugh derisively and call her a hopeless tax-and-spend Massachusetts liberal?

_____B. Explain that the poor could get rich, too, if they were smart enough to figure out how to set up an offshore tax shelter?

_____C. Tell her that if she doesn't like her tax cut she should donate it to the North American Man-Boy Love Association or some other liberal charity?

_____D. Argue that giving money back to the people who pay the highest taxes will help to spur investment and create jobs that benefit the economy as a whole?

2. You're showing off your gun collection to your new neighbor, and you discover that he's a staunch gun-control advocate. He says that guns endanger everyone's lives. Do you:

_____A. "Accidentally" blow off his foot?

_____B. Explain that guns don't kill people, only dangerous minorities do?

_____C. Pull out a copy of the Second Amendment and ask him to read it out loud and identify which words he doesn't understand?

_____D. Explain that you've had extensive training in gun safety and offer to take him hunting?

3. A friend confesses after Bible study that she's thinking of voting for a Democrat in the next election. Do you:

_____A. Wish her well on her journey to the fiery pits of everlasting hell?

_____B. Bind her with duct tape and force her to watch FOX News until she regains a fair and balanced viewpoint?

_____C. Warn her about the liberal plot to wage war on Christmas, Easter, and Flag Day?

_____D. Challenge her with tough questions and demonstrate how voting that way is not in her self-interest?

If you answered D to all of the previous questions, you're ready to move on to the next section. If not, this may help explain why you haven't been winning many arguments lately (and possibly why you don't get invited to social functions anymore).

Your voice is like a jackal picking at my brain! I hate you! I hate who you are and what you do and how you sound and what you say! You're like a cancer on my life!

—Stephen Colbert, arguing with Steve Carell on *The Daily Show*

How Not to Be an Asshole

Tempted as you may be to blurt out obscenities, hurl insults, or pepper-spray your opponent, successful arguing strategy (and the laws of polite society) require that you employ more civilized tactics. The following chart will show you how to channel your fury in a way that, while being admittedly less satisfying than, say, telling your opponent to go perform an anatomical sexual impossibility, will help encourage better diplomatic relations.

What You'll Be Tempted to Say	How to Translate That into Diplo-Speak
"Are you completely freaking insane?"	"I'm not sure I'm following the reasoning behind your argument."
"Did your lobotomy leave a scar?"	"Do you honestly believe that?"
"Which dark crevice of your ass did you pull that from?"	"How do you back up that claim?"
"Stupid hippie weasel."	"I can't identify with what you're saying."
"What do the demons say when they come for you at night?"	"How did you arrive at that conclusion?"
"Do I need to speak slower with fewer syllables?"	"I'm not sure we're communicating."

What You'll Be Tempted to Say	How to Translate That into Diplo-Speak
"I've never met a bigger phony in my life."	"Nice to meet you, Mrs. Pelosi."
"Isn't it great that we live in a country where even a total douchebag like yourself is free to utter whatever mindless drivel pops into his head?"	"You have a right to your opinion."
"Shut up and fly the flag!"	"There must be something we can agree on."
"I'd rather be driven over a rickety bridge by Ted Kennedy than listen to another word you have to say."	"I think we're going to have to agree to disagree."

THE TEN COMMANDMENTS OF PARTISAN WARFARE

Here is your guide to becoming a model partisan.

1. KEEP IT SIMPLE

A long-winded, nuanced, complex argument is a guaranteed ticket to disaster. Just ask John Kerry or Al Gore or Michael Dukakis. To be effective, you need to be able to fit your basic message on a bumper sticker.

2. PERSONALIZE THE ISSUE

Don't talk about issues in an abstract way. Persuade by talking in terms of how issues affect people, relate your own experiences, and highlight your opponent's self-interest (e.g., show them how Republican policies mean more money in their pocket, more personal freedom, and more jokes from the likes of Jon Stewart and Stephen Colbert, at the expense of Republicans).

3. FRAME THE ARGUMENT TO YOUR ADVANTAGE

Make your case by presenting each issue according to your own beliefs and values, *not theirs*. Never, for example, let a sanctimonious liberal elitist lecture you about values or the meaning of tolerance. If you let them frame the debate, they win (more on that later in this chapter).

4. FIND COMMON GROUND

Build your street cred with liberals by bad-mouthing a despised conservative—say, Ann Coulter or Pat Robertson. That way you'll defy stereotypes and demonstrate that your allegiances are not blind. Continue to rope them in by appealing to shared values and common interests before unleashing your Trojan horse–style sneak attack.

5. EXPOSE HYPOCRISY

Nothing undermines an argument faster than exposing hypocritical behavior, contradictory statements, and wholesale fakery—either on the part of your opponents or the politicians they're defending. There are few sights as satisfying as watching exposed hypocrites grasp at fig leaves to cover their shame.

6. EXUDE CONFIDENCE

Always project the courage of your convictions. Like bees and dogs, your opponent can smell fear and weakness. *How* you say something is just as important as *what* you say.

7. DON'T SERMONIZE:

No one likes to be lectured to, and no one likes a self-righteous windbag. Ranting from atop your soapbox will only harden your opponent's position and make him or her more hostile. If you've made an enemy, you haven't won an argument.

8. MAKE YOUR OPPONENT LAUGH

Humor can be a potent weapon in political debate. Making humorous observations—and demonstrating an ability to laugh at yourself—will help disarm your opponents and keep them engaged. If funny isn't your thing, quote professional quipsters like Dennis Miller or unintentional comedians like Howard Dean.

9. BE OPEN-MINDED

It's the civility, stupid. Be prepared to listen respectfully and concede a point or two before moving in for the kill. You can learn a lot from people with whom you disagree—even those you believe to be outrageously misguided—and fine-tune your arguments in the process.

10. PICK BATTLES YOU CAN WIN

Don't expend too much energy trying to win over a staunch liberal. You'd have better luck trying to coax a rock to grow. Target the fence-sitters and the more easily converted. It's a strategy that has worked for religious missionaries for centuries, and it can work for you.

HOW TO FRAME THE DEBATE USING SIMPLE JEDI MIND TRICKS

To win a political argument, you must control the terms of debate. If you let your adversary define the terms and frame the discussion, you lose.

Most conservatives have an intuitive sense of how to frame their arguments because they see liberalism as the root of most of the country's problems (a point, by the way, which can be fun to watch liberals try and refute). Liberals, on the other hand, are generally so busy itemizing their grievances with the world, focus-grouping their principles, or arguing with themselves, that they have a hard enough time figuring out what arguments they even believe, let alone how to frame them.

The key to successful framing is to 1. keep your eye on the big picture; 2. stay on the offensive; 3. don't get sidetracked trying to refute every liberal lie or distortion; 4. tie your argument into a broader narrative; and 5. never, under any circumstances— even if abducted by naked hippies and forced to lie down in the sand to help them spell out "Impeach Bush"—let liberals frame the debate on their own terms.

The handy thing about this approach is that it can be just as effective on the strong-willed as the weak-minded. Here are two examples of how to handle a debate on religion; the first is badly botched, the second smartly framed.

Liberal blowhard: *I'll tell you what's wrong with this country—it's all the intolerant religious nutcases who are trying to impose their radical Pat Robertson agenda on everyone. They've declared a jihad against gay people, feminists, sex, stem cells, pro-choice supporters, and the rest of us so-called unwashed heathens who don't buy into their medieval worldview. Our country is being torn apart by Bible-beating bigots.*

Untrained conservative: *Since when is it a crime to speak out against sin? You can demonize the religious faithful all you want, but the Bible makes it perfectly clear that homosexuality, premarital sex, and taking innocent life are all sins, despite whatever the abortionists, feminazis, or Brokeback Mountaineers may have told you.*

Liberal blowhard: *Look, the point is, if we let the religious fanatics have their way, pretty soon we'll all be living in a theocracy run by our very own Christian Taliban.*

Untrained conservative: *It beats living in a society where sexually permissive liberal deviants like you give sanction to everything from gay marriage to man-on-dog sex.*

Notice how the untrained conservative takes the bait that plays right into their hands by fighting on liberals' turf? By being purely reactive, the untrained conservative loses from the outset. Contrast that to the smarter conservative, who seizes control of the discussion and reframes it around a theme that works to her advantage.

Smarter conservative: *Funny you should talk about tolerance because religious tolerance happens to be one of the cornerstones of our democracy—and of conservatism. Our country was founded on principles of religious freedom by people who were persecuted and demonized as religious nutcases by the ACLUs and People for the American Ways of their day. That's why we have a little thing in this country called the First Amendment, which guarantees freedom of religion, not freedom from religion. Instead of trying to silence people who hold different views, wouldn't the tolerant position be to respect their right to free speech and free religious exercise without going all exorcist on them?*

We'll show you how to frame more arguments in Chapter Seven, but you get the idea.

How to Avoid Unhinged Lunatics

There's nothing wrong with occasionally mixing it up with liberals who have extreme views. It's the ones who have extreme personality disorders that you should be concerned about. You know, those totally incapable of having an intelligent, thoughtful discussion about anything. They bicker instead of argue, rant instead of talk, and parrot instead of think.

These kinds of sociopaths can be found anywhere—ambushing perfect strangers at cocktail parties, accosting hapless victims at neighborhood barbecues, even holding entire families hostage at holiday time in hopes of spewing their claptrap with impunity.

There is no use wasting perfectly good oxygen arguing with these people. You'll be much better off—and cut down on your Xanax bills—if you focus your energies on reasonable people capable of passing a Field Sanity Test. Here's how to administer it:

> ★ Do they become instantly irate at the slightest of triggers? For example, if you just say

the word "Bush," does their face turn visibly red and do their neck veins begin pulsating?

★ In place of the usual expletives, do they use "FOX," "Cheney," "Scalia," "Boehner," or "Halliburton"?

★ Do they display a pathological fear of opposing viewpoints? For example, do they proudly restrict their intake of news and information to what they read on left-wing blogs, the message board at their local food co-op, or the pamphlets they were handed at the last Green Antiglobalization S&M Festival?

★ Are they prone to Tourette's-like outbursts, in which they spasmodically denounce you as a "stupid evil Nazi," "ignorant inbred redneck," or "extra-chromosome, slack-jawed troglodyte"?

★ Do they show signs of cognitive impairment? For example, can they be seen attending an antiwar rally, hoisting a sign that says "U.S. Out of My Uterus!" without even realizing they're in the wrong place?

★ Do they have the same stock answer to everything? For example, do they frequently explain that conservatives simply love war-mongering, torturing, outsourcing, election stealing, or biting the heads off of puppies?

★ Do they currently or have they ever anchored the *CBS Evening News*?

If the liberal in question exhibits any of these behavior patterns, he or she has failed the Field Sanity Test. Do yourself a favor—back away slowly and avoid these people as you would a Hillary Clinton campaign rally. Nothing good will ever come of talking to them.

Anyone else is fair game.

★ **CHAPTER 5** ★

How to Win Friends While Antagonizing People

LUKE: Your thoughts betray you, Father. I feel the good in you, the conflict.

DARTH VADER: There is no conflict.

LUKE: You couldn't bring yourself to kill me before, and I don't believe you'll destroy me now.

DARTH VADER: You underestimate the power of the Dark Side. If you will not fight, then you will meet your destiny.

—*Star Wars: Return of the Jedi*

Everyone says you shouldn't argue politics in polite company. But where's the fun in that? You have to hone your combat skills somewhere. And who better to prey on than your friends and loved ones or the guy in the next cubicle?

Navigating these minefields, however, requires special training. To help you bait and baffle your adversaries (while avoiding interpersonal disaster), this chapter offers some essential "DOs" and "DON'Ts" for dealing with several potentially hazardous combat zones.

How to Survive Family Sparring Matches

For some families it's an annual ritual: Everyone is sitting around the dinner table, enjoying a lovely Thanksgiving meal and getting into the holiday spirit, when Uncle Blowhard says, "Speaking of things we have to be thankful for, I'm thankful that Americans had the good sense to bounce out the Republican Congress and hold Bush accountable for his atrocities."

Cousin Jodi takes the bait and says, "Do you want the *terrorists* to win?" Pretty soon the conversation descends into a back-and-forth volley of pronouncements, such as, "If you're so gung-ho about war, go enlist!" and "Why don't you move to Canada!" At which point chairs are pushed back and dishes are cleared, while your mother weeps quietly in the corner.

The thing about arguing with family is, you're in it for the long haul. That gives you a little more leeway, so everyone knows they can push the envelope further than they would in other situations. For that reason, a few basic rules apply.

★ **DON'T** let Uncle Blowhard hold the dinner table hostage. Fact-check him right then and there, using the Internet browser on your BlackBerry or cell phone. Counter him point-for-point, fire off contradictory statistics, and apply duct tape as needed. Remember, liberals hate facts. They get in the way of oversimplifications. It's like sunlight to a vampire.

★ **DON'T** proselytize to your children about your politics; they'll just rebel. First they'll start experimenting by privately reading liberal blogs, and then progress to social use of Democratic talking points. The next thing you know they'll have developed a habitual dependency on liberal dogma, for which there may be no rehabilitation.

★ **DON'T** try to get in the last word with a liberal loved one at his or her own funeral. It comes off as insensitive to stand over a deceased liberal saying, "See what happens when you reject Bush as your Savior" or, "Let's see if that affirmative action plan helps get you into heaven now."

★ **DO** crack jokes to disarm your opponents and lull them into a false sense of complacency. Keep an ample supply of alcohol at the ready, or better yet, ply them with coffee or Red Bull (people who are wired on caffeine are more susceptible to persuasion, according to an actual scientific study).

★ **DO** attempt to recruit impressionable family members to your side, particularly when they're young; for example, give your seven-year-old nephew a $100 bill and explain that he should keep it in a safe place, because one day liberals will try to take it away.

★ **DO** consider holding an intervention if you are truly worried about a family member's well-being—for example, if that same nephew later considers attending a liberal arts college in the northeast because it offers courses such as The Sexuality of Terrorism and Marxist Cinema.

Well, there was no sex for fourteen days.

—California Governor Arnold Schwarzenegger, on how his wife, Maria Shriver (of Kennedy clan fame), reacted after he gave a speech praising President Bush at the 2004 Republican Convention

WHAT TO DO IF YOU'RE SLEEPING WITH THE ENEMY

Love makes people do crazy things, and chief among them is dating (or even marrying) your political enemy. Many households have their own partisan divides. He listens to Rush Limbaugh; she listens to NPR. He decides who to vote for based on the candidate he'd most like to drink beer with; she goes with the person she'd rather trust performing brain surgery. He's a serpent-headed Democratic strategist known as the Ragin' Cajun; she's a sharp-tongued Republican strategist and confidant of Dick Cheney.

Some mixed couples manage to coexist in a state of harmony. For others, it ends with a restraining order. Consider the case of one couple in Georgia who made headlines after the woman informed her boyfriend, a Marine recruit, that she was leaving him *and* voting for John Kerry. That's when he tried to stab her repeatedly with a screwdriver. "You'll never live to see the election," he told her before officers subdued him with a taser gun.

To help you remain faithful to both your beliefs and your significant other (while keeping yourself out of jail), here are a few pointers.

★ **DON'T** engage in any sort of political discussion with your opposite-ideological partner if you're hoping to get laid afterward. Wait until after the sex. Five minutes is not going to kill you. Remember, if you're having sex correctly, you won't have the energy for the argument to get out of hand. (If perchance the sex was unprotected, now would be a good time to discuss your opposition to abortion.)

★ **DON'T** resort to amateurish passive-aggressive behavior, such as lining the birdcage with your honey's absentee ballot. Instead, take it up a notch—host an NRA party and use her old Barbra Streisand LPs for skeet shooting.

★ **DON'T** let resentments fester; if you're still bitter about the volunteer work she did for the Al Sharpton 2004 campaign, it's time to let it go.

★ **DON'T** kid yourself; if you discover a tote bag containing baggy fatigues, a crowbar, a gas mask, and a bundle of antiglobalization leaflets, pack up the kids and head for the nearest red state.

★ **DO** tease your significant other about how she is really a Republican deep down. (How else to explain the Schwarzenegger DVD collection or the fact that Donald Rumsfeld is on her celebrity sex list?)

★ **DO** compromise; if she insists on listening to Air America Radio while you're driving around, put a "Stop Global Whining" bumper sticker on the car.

★ **DO** consider withholding sex to make a political point, but only if you're capable of holding out (guys, please skip on to the next tip). If that doesn't work, try withholding gadgets or restricting his PlayStation or TiVo privileges.

★ **DO** agree on a safeword to signal when you've reached your limit, like people do with S&M. If she's extolling the virtues of raising taxes to pay for new prescription drug benefits, shout "eightball," "bananas," or "Greenspan," and take a time-out.

HOW TO MANAGE WORKPLACE SQUABBLES

During the course of their adult lives, most Americans are doomed to spend about one-third of every waking hour toiling in the workplace. Whether you're looking for a political argument or not, you're bound to find yourself mixing it up with a liberal colleague sooner or later. Because workplace arguments can be a serious occupational hazard, here are some tips that will help you serve your partisan cause while holding onto your job at the same time.

★ **DON'T** get into a political spat with your boss or anyone else above your pay grade; it's hard to beat the argument "You're fired!"

★ **DON'T** be a stalker, like that guy in accounting who's always cornering people, ranting about which countries should be nuked, and trying to get you to read his MySpace blog; no one likes that guy.

★ **DON'T** plaster your workspace with annoying propaganda or signage (e.g., stickers that say "Kick Their Ass and Take Their Gas," "I Love Gitmo," or that photo of you patrolling the Mexican border with the Minute Men). It signals you're either desperate for attention or huffing liquid paper. In either case, your coworkers will avoid you. Note: This "don't" is even more important if you share your cubicle with your Beanie Baby™ collection and photos of your six cats.

★ **DO** form alliances with like-minded colleagues; a coordinated assault around the water cooler by a coalition of the willing is always better than going it alone. You can even pass resolutions and impose sanctions against rogue departments.

★ **DO** consider playing psychological warfare; convince a liberal colleague that you're actually a liberal too, win his or her trust, and then at a crucial moment—say, right before Election Day—express your total disillusionment with the Democratic Party and convince your colleague to join you in abandoning ship.

★ **DO** make sure to participate in departmental birthday celebrations. You'll get free cake, and when the liberal's card is passed around, you can write an eloquent birthday wish and sign it "Rudy Giuliani." Who isn't going to vote for someone who wrote nice things on their birthday card?

★ **DO** turn a difference of opinion into a friendly wager. If you win a bet about Republicans winning the upcoming election, for example, your coworker has to agree to wear a tie with elephants on it at all staff meetings for one year.

How to Clash with Perfect Strangers

A few days after the 2004 presidential election, a pugnacious liberal posted on Craigslist.org in Washington, D.C. the following anonymous message: "I would like to fight a Bush supporter to vent my anger. If you are one, [and] have a fiery streak, please contact me so we can meet and physically fight. I would like to beat the shit out of you."

Another Craigslist poster offered a similar proposition: "Any of you Republicans want to fight? Street brawl, bodies only, no weapons. I will not be merciful. I'm sick of this tough-guy shit. Let's see what you got."

Going around and picking fights with strangers is generally not recommended. However, there are a few situations where *verbally* mixing it up with strangers may be warranted, perhaps even imperative. Here are a few guidelines.

★ **DON'T** antagonize anyone who may be able to take advantage of you in a compromising situation, such as your hairstylist, skydiving instructor, plastic surgeon, anesthesiologist, or the guy making your burrito.

★ **DON'T** engage in fisticuffs with liberals; they'll curl into the fetal position before you can even land a punch, and then slap you with a lawsuit claiming emotional distress.

★ **DON'T** get into an argument with the liberal sitting next to you on an airplane. There won't be enough barf bags on hand to stop him from hyperventilating and sucking up all the oxygen. And worse, you'll have no exit strategy.

★ **DO** feel free to mix it up with petition gatherers, pamphleteers, and other partisan stalkers; the longer you hold them hostage, the less time they'll have to disperse their propaganda.

★ **DO** crash antiwar rallies and make a point to taunt protesters; if you can provoke a violent outburst from just one peace-loving hippie, it will make for amusing news coverage.

★ **DO** feel free to heckle any celebrity performer who decides to launch into an obnoxious anti-Republican tirade while you're sitting in the audience. The next time somebody pulls a Dixie Chick on you, shout them down by calling them brainless

French-fellating appeasers, godless troop-slandering pansies, or any other combination of insults. If you happen to be carrying lighter fluid for just such an event, a post-concert CD-burning bonfire can be a great way to meet new friends.

HOW TO PROPERLY ENGAGE IN INTERNET FLAME WARS

If you've never been denounced as a bedwetting, fascist, crack-addicted, terrorist crybaby by dozens of people you've never met, you've never experienced the joys of an Internet flame war. For the uninitiated, this is where you post messages in any type of online forum and engage in a flaming back-and-forth war of words that would generally be considered unacceptable in polite society.

There are two key advantages in engaging in this type of political discourse: 1. You get to deploy all the anti-liberal epithets and denunciations that have been swirling in your mind; and 2. it's all anonymous, which means there's no need to lose any sleep over the taunts or threats that will inevitably be issued against you.

If you plan to get involved in a flame war, here are a few things to keep in mind. Note that some of the tips here run counter to the advice offered elsewhere in the book. That's the whole point of flame wars. It is the Internet, after all. Normal rules of decorum need not apply.

★ **DON'T** call your opponent a Nazi. That's so twentieth century. Instead, use terms like digital Bolshevik, cyber Trotskyite, Marxist troll, and, where appropriate, batshit-crazy, genocidal douche bag.

★ **DON'T** ever provide any real information about yourself. It's more fun to pretend to be someone you're not—a mid-level Homeland Security official, for example, who is carefully monitoring everything they're saying.

★ **DON'T** get overly worked up or spend too much time flaming. If you're missing meals or forgetting to shower, you've got a problem. That's valuable time you could use for more productive pursuits, like trying to hack Michael Moore's website or signing up the staff of MoveOn.org for military recruiting emails.

★ **DO** feel free to invent your own facts. If pressed for evidence, simply create your own Wikipedia entry to support your arguments. There are plenty of Wikipidiots out there who will believe anything they read on the Net.

★ **DO** take high personal offense to anything you can. Explain, for example, that you lost an arm, a leg, and an eye in the War on Christmas and you're outraged by their callous insensitivity to your religious beliefs. Inform them that you've been slandered and they'll be hearing from your lawyer.

★ **DO** demonstrate that you are on the cutting edge of Internet discourse by using expletives such as "asshat," "assclown," and "ignoranus." Bonus points: If you use the number "3" instead of the letter "e" and "P" in place of "O," you'll confuse the piss out of them and let them know they've been "Pwn3d! LOL!"

CHAPTER 6

Advanced Battle Tactics

The enemy isn't liberalism. The enemy isn't conservatism. The enemy is bullshit.

—Lars-Erik Nelson

To triumph in battle, you need to be prepared to deal with devious adversaries. As you probably well know, many liberals are highly skilled in the dark arts of manipulation. They bullshit with abandon and commit grotesque crimes against logic as a force of habit.

In this chapter, we'll show you how to cut through that nonsense. We'll help you hone your Bullshit Detector, anticipate bogus lines of attack, and exploit weaknesses in your opponents' arguments so you can force them to engage in a more honest debate—or shut them up entirely.

To round out your training, we'll provide some advanced-level tips for seasoned combatants and show you how to turn even the bleakest of situations into a moral victory.

How to Detect Bullshit

Let's state the obvious. Liberals love to bullshit. We're not just talking about the professionals in Washington. Your average liberal on the street is skilled at slinging it too.

To combat bullshit, it's important to first define what it is and what makes it so insidious. "Bullshit is a greater enemy of the truth than lies are," says Harry Frankfurt, who literally wrote the book *On Bullshit*. A bullshitter, Frankfurt says, is distinguished by the fact that he couldn't care less about whether what he is saying is true. He has a completely different agenda. A bullshitter is mainly concerned with trying to wow, distract, or manipulate his audience, and he'll simply cherry-pick facts or make things up to fit his needs.

That's why bullshitters are such menaces to society: Their total lack of regard for the truth gives them free rein to manipulate people willy-nilly, so long as no one calls them on it.

They also have one thing in common: They're trying to conceal something. To help you calibrate your Bullshit Detector, here's a guide to the various bullshitting life forms that you are likely to encounter and what they are trying to hide.

THE KNOWLEDGE SUPREMACISTS

What they do: They attempt to dazzle their audiences with their sheer volume of knowledge on any given topic. Their goal is to use that knowledge as a trump card to assert their superior opinions, based on having access to information you are lacking.

What they're hiding: Their intellectual inferiority complex.

THE CREDENTIAL FALSIFIERS

What they do: They claim to have unique life experiences or qualifications that you don't, and which, therefore, validate their views and negate yours. For example, they may refer to their military training and combat experience when it turns out that all they ever did was play paintball.

What they're hiding: The fact that they're average and ill-informed.

THE FACT SPINNERS

What they do: They present you with the "straight facts," which, on closer examination, turn out to be wrong, distorted, taken out of context, or spun to suit their agenda. When faced with inconvenient facts, they create a smokescreen of doubt by either questioning the source (e.g., crying foul over so-called "conservative media bias") or declaring the facts open to debate.

What they're hiding: That they no longer know the difference between fact and fiction, and worse, they don't care.

THE "TRUTHINESS" TELLERS

What they do: They cling to the truths that come straight from their gut, rather than reality. As defined by comedian Stephen Colbert, "truthiness" refers to an individual's preference for believing in what he or she wishes to be true rather than what is known to be true.

What they're hiding: Their utter terror of reality.

THE BULLSHIT ACOLYTES

What they do: They perpetuate left-wing spin through empty sloganeering and mindless repetition of Democratic talking points crafted by the likes of Al Franken, Michael Moore, and George Soros.

What they're hiding: The fact that they can't think for themselves.

How to Trip Up a Bullshitter

Good bullshitters can be hard to spot, but you may be able to trip them up by their failure to answer basic questions or inability to support their claims. Next time you smell the stink, take the following steps.

1. Hit them with simple questions, such as, "How do you know that?" "How can you prove that?" or, if you've got a firm fix on the issue, "How do you account for the fact that *The New York Times*, NPR, and Oprah herself completely contradict everything you just said?"

2. If you suspect they're just blindly spewing rhetoric or unthinkingly parroting left-wing spin, challenge them to provide specifics. For example, make them explain exactly how leaving the battlefield helps us fight terrorists, how specifically the media has a conservative bias, or how precisely Halliburton intends to take over the world.

3. As they grasp to substantiate their claims, watch for telltale signs of lying, such as lack of eye contact, a scratch to the nose or chin, compulsive lip-licking, dilated pupils, or sweating through their hemp shirt. Consider responses such as "I read it in a Daily Kos discussion thread," "I heard it at a MoveOn.org house party," or "Because Al Gore said so" to be inadequate defenses.

4. Call them on their deceit, show them where they went wrong, and suggest that they leave the

bullshitting to trained professionals, like Howard Dean discoursing on national security, Nancy Pelosi sermonizing on mainstream values, or Bill Clinton pontificating on a stewardess.

HOW TO SPOT LOGICAL FALLACIES

If you've ever been part of an argument that feels disingenuous, grossly oversimplified, rigged against you, or which makes no earthly sense, then you've probably encountered a logical fallacy. They're the three-legged stools of faulty reasoning that liberals rely on to prop up many of their ridiculous ideas.

Some liberals deliberately use logical fallacies to play manipulative mind games, while others may inadvertently stick a finger in the eye of reason. Whatever the case, learning to recognize common logical fallacies—and calling your opponent on them—will help you to immediately deflate many bogus lines of attack. Or, if you're feeling Machiavellian, you can use these techniques to pull a fast one on an unwitting opponent.

HASTY GENERALIZATION

Jumping to a far-reaching conclusion based on scant evidence or forming a stereotype based on a single flimsy example or two.

Example: "Conservatives love to rail against gay marriage and rhapsodize about family values, but they're all a bunch of closeted hypocrites who like to prey on young boys and bed down with gay hookers. Just look at Mark Foley and Reverend Ted Haggard."

APPEAL TO AUTHORITY

Invoking an authority figure—whether a politician, a journalist, or a famous person—to prove an argument rather than substantiating the argument itself.

Example: "Of course, Barack Obama is the right man for the job. He's been endorsed by George Clooney, Alec Baldwin, Whoopi Goldberg, and former president Martin Sheen."

FALSE CHOICE

Offering only two options for consideration when there are clearly other valid choices.

Example: "Either we raise taxes on the wealthy to balance the budget or we keep cutting taxes and watch the deficit spiral out of control faster than the Bush twins at a tequila bar."

STRAWMAN

Oversimplifying, exaggerating, caricaturing, or otherwise misrepresenting your position without regard to fact. In doing this, your opponent sets up a figurative strawman that he can easily knock down to prove his point.

Example: "Maybe you think it's just to wage war for oil in hopes of bringing on the apocalypse so that you can be raptured to heaven. But sane people understand that the Iraq war was a mistake."

APPEAL TO FEAR

Preying on people's fears in an attempt to skirt any need for evidence or analysis about an issue.

Example: "If you don't do your part to stop global warming by installing compact fluorescent lightbulbs, the ice caps are going to melt and turn your living room into a well-lit aquarium."

THE BANDWAGON APPEAL

Demonstrating that an argument is valid based on the fact that it is popularly accepted or because "everyone is doing it."

Example: "Most Americans believe, as I do, that we should allow medicinal marijuana, so why are we even debating this when we should be calling your old roommate Dave to get him to write us a prescription?"

AD HOMINEN

Leveling a personal attack in an attempt to discredit an argument rather than addressing the argument itself.

Example: "I would like to apologize for referring to George W. Bush as a 'deserter.' What I meant to say is that George W. Bush is a deserter, an election thief, a drunk driver, a WMD liar, and a functional illiterate. And he poops his pants."
—Michael Moore

SLIPPERY SLOPE

Leaping to wild, sometimes inexplicable conclusions—going, say, from Step 1 to Step 2 and then all the way to Step 10 without establishing any discernible connection. By using this kind of leapfrog logic, a person can come to any conclusion he damn well pleases.

Example: "First we had the Patriot Act, then warrantless wiretapping, and then the suspension of habeas corpus. If Republicans keep using the Constitution as toilet paper, pretty soon we'll be living in a fascist police state."

FALSE CAUSE

This fallacy, known among logic buffs as *post hoc ergo propter hoc,* based on the assertion that because one action or event occurs and is followed by another, the first must have caused the second.

Example: "President Bush came into office in 2001, and eight months later we were attacked by terrorists. I rest my case."

Other Common Liberal Fallacies

The Moorian Fallacy: an illogical argument made over a period of ninety minutes in a documentary film format

The Clintonian Phallacy: a self-deluding logical contortion used to rationalize why the fat, ugly chick you banged was worth risking your career over

Ad Franken: a fallacious argument told in the form of a joke (caveat: joke may not actually be funny)

Argumentum Ad Hollywood: an illogical argument made by a Hollywood idiot during a nationally televised award acceptance speech, based on the fallacious assumption that anyone cares what they think

"STRATEGERY" FOR THE ADVANCED COMBATANT

Your liberal opponents are likely to rely on deceitful and underhanded tactics, so you'll need to stay one step ahead. Here are a few winning plays and ploys you can use to outmaneuver your opponent and give yourself maximum advantage in any political argument.

ANTICIPATE YOUR OPPONENTS' ARGUMENTS

You can gain a tactical advantage by familiarizing yourself with your opponents' arguments and understanding why they make them.

Your mission: You'll have to occasionally brave the unspeakable horrors of reading their crazy magazines, opinion columns, and blogs, listening to their talk-radio squawkers, watching the Clinton News Network, and even subjecting yourself to the torture of Nancy Pelosi news conferences.

Upshot: If you're not acquainted with the latest fashions in liberal thought, you won't fully appreciate how insane they actually are.

ASK POINTED QUESTIONS THAT WILL BOX IN YOUR OPPONENT

One of the most effective arguing techniques, utilized by lawyers and others skilled in the persuasion arts, simply involves posing a series of questions. It's known as the Socratic method, and it's easy to employ.

Your mission: Start by getting your opponents to answer broad questions about their beliefs and then, as you narrow down to the specific issue at hand, look to expose inconsistencies or contradictions. For example, ask if fairness is a core value of liberalism. Ask if it's fair to discriminate against a group of people by denying them the same opportunities that are available to other people. Then ask if affirmative action policies that have punished a generation of white people by giving preferential treatment to minorities are, in fact, fair.

Upshot: You make your opponents defeat themselves.

ANSWER THE QUESTION YOU WISH YOU'D BEEN ASKED

Many liberals will ask you dumb, leading, or nonsensical questions to try to trap you. You don't have to play that game when you can recast the question in a way that works to your advantage—a simple little trick politicians use every day.

Your mission: When a liberal asks something like, "How do you square your support with a culture of life with the fact that as many as a half million innocent Iraqis have been killed in the war?" you answer this way: "Any loss of innocent human life is obviously a tragedy. But the question is, how many more lives might have been lost if we failed to fight an aggressive war on terror? How many innocent Americans would be killed if we failed to protect ourselves against the sick fanatics who would blow up every last American city if they had the chance?"

Upshot: You remain on the offensive, frame the debate as you want to, and avoid liberals' attempts to place you in a rhetorical straightjacket.

NEVER USE LIBERALS' WORDS

Liberals love to use phrases like "undocumented workers," "pro-choice," "anti-choice," and "alternative lifestyles" to spin their various positions. The worst thing you can do is to repeat them. As conservative language guru Frank Luntz says, "When you use the words of your opposition, you are basically accepting their definition and therefore their conclusion."

Your mission: When liberals refer to "undocumented workers," correct them by referring to "illegal aliens." When they whine about "domestic surveillance," call it "terrorist surveillance." When they call for "troop redeployment" in Iraq, term it "surrendering."

Upshot: By beating your opponents at their own word game, you put them on the defensive while exposing the lie behind their inane babble.

USE WEDGE ISSUES

Republicans have been using wedge issues to drive a stake through liberals' hearts for years. Abortion, gay marriage, flag burning, and gun control are all examples of how divisive issues can be used to highlight fundamental differences between liberals and conservatives.

Your mission: Instead of turning to the most radioactive wedges, try a few less divisive issues that have greater potential to win you converts, such as liberals' soft stance on terrorist interrogations, illegal immigration, or the gratuitous violence, indiscriminate sex, and misogynistic music that the entertainment industry is peddling to our kids like crack.

Upshot: You'll keep your opponents on the defensive and, if you're lucky, help a few would-be Democratic voters see the error of their ways.

SHINE A LIGHT ON LIBERAL MOONBATS

From the drunken liberal congressman who runs his car into a concrete barrier on Capitol Hill to your average liberal on the street who tries to run over a Republican congresswoman with his car, crazy liberals are not hard to find.

Your mission: Make a point of highlighting every moronic Hollywood celebrity utterance, every liberal sexual shenanigan, or every drunken Kennedy family exploit to illustrate the true face of liberalism (see Chapter Eight: The Liberal Hall of Shame).

Upshot: The more you tie liberalism to its most unhinged extremists, the more unsavory the entire liberal philosophy becomes for nonpsychotic adherents. All you need to do is shine the light and back away.

How to Argue Like a Liberal in Fourteen Easy Steps

If you've ever wondered why arguing with liberals feels a lot like banging your head against a wall, it's because their debating strategy typically follows this basic pattern:

1. Blame America
2. Play the victim
3. Blame FOX News
4. Play race card (especially when you're white)
5. Lump ten unrelated issues together
6. Blame corporations
7. Propose inventive new ways to spend other people's money
8. Mock people of faith
9. Blame Bush for everything from gas prices to not being able to get a date on eHarmony.com
10. Compare Republicans to Nazis
11. Guilt-trip their opponents about their insensitive "hate speech"
12. Congratulate themselves for being so tolerant
13. Change the subject
14. Rinse and repeat

I argue very well. Ask any of my remaining friends. I can win an argument on any topic, against any opponent. People know this, and steer clear of me at parties. Often, as a sign of their great respect, they don't even invite me.

—Dave Barry

How to Win When You Can't Win Them Over

As a passionate partisan who's determined to convert liberals to your way of thinking, you want what anyone would want: to watch them grovel on their knees as they recant their beliefs and praise you for showing them the path to salvation. But short of shipping them off to Guantanamo for reeducation, it's safe to say the odds of that happening are slim.

The reality is that you can do everything right, make flawless arguments, and still find yourself getting nowhere, your head throbbing with that dull concussive feeling that comes from butting your head against a wall of steel-reinforced ignorance. Fortunately, there are several other important ways in which you can still declare victory when you haven't won them over. You can chug a celebratory beer if you succeed in doing any of the following.

HUMILIATE YOUR OPPONENT

If you can undercut your opponent's arguments while making him look foolish in the process, you may not win a convert, but you can emancipate yourself—and perhaps a few grateful bystanders— from their bullshit.

BREAK STEREOTYPES

You can do a lot to mess with liberals' minds simply by presenting yourself as a thoughtful conservative who cares about her country and makes intelligent, reasoned arguments. That way, the next time they try to say that all conservatives are a bunch of intolerant, knuckle-dragging religious freaks, the wholly unfamiliar part of their brain known as their conscience will alert them to the fact that they're lying. Some liberals obviously won't have a problem with this, but others will be forced to make accommodations to the unwanted intrusion of reality.

SHAKE THEIR CONFIDENCE IN THE DEMOCRATIC PARTY

You may not be able to persuade people that their views are wrong, but you may be able to show them that their party is not representing their views. You can score a victory by highlighting the many ways in which the Democratic Party has moved too far to the left in service to its antiwar, big government–promoting, class warfare–waging base. To paraphrase Ronald Reagan, show them that they haven't left the party, but their party has left them.

SOW YOUR OPPONENT WITH SEEDS OF SELF-DOUBT

If your opponent gives you everything he's got and then finds himself trapped under the weight of his own inadequacy—making fruitless counterarguments or being reduced to speechlessness—that's a good time to walk away. Let him fester in his own silent insufficiency. One day those seeds may bloom into giant flowers of debilitating self-doubt.

WIN OVER THE CROWD

When you're arguing with a liberal in front of other people—at a dinner party, for example—you can score a major victory simply by making superior arguments. Your goal is to appear more knowledgeable, more reasonable, and more logical while exposing your opponent as ill-prepared, hypocritical, or simply clueless. Do that and it doesn't matter whether you win over your adversary because you will have won the crowd.

PREVAIL IN A WAR OF ATTRITION

You may not be able to bring someone around overnight, but with patience and persistence, and possibly with the help of enough alcohol, you may eventually break your opponent down and get her to admit the folly of her ways—or at least stop voting for Democrats.

How to Argue Like a Spin Doctor

In the film *Thank You for Smoking*, a tobacco lobbyist (Nick) and his son (Joey) discuss arguing strategy:

Nick: Let's say that you're defending chocolate, and I'm defending vanilla. Now, if I were to say to you 'Vanilla is the best flavor ice cream,' you'd say . . .

Joey: 'No, chocolate is.'

Nick: Exactly. But you can't win that argument. So, I'll ask you, 'So you think chocolate is the end-all and be-all of ice cream, do you?'

Joey: It's the best ice cream. I wouldn't order any other.

Nick: Oh. So it's all chocolate for you, is it?

Joey: Yes, chocolate is all I need.

Nick: Well, I need more than chocolate. And for that matter, I need more than vanilla. I believe that we need freedom and choice when it comes to our ice cream, and that . . . is the definition of liberty.

Joey: But that's not what we're talking about.

Nick: Ah. But that's what I'm talking about.

Joey: But . . . you didn't prove that vanilla's the best.

Nick: I didn't have to. I proved that you're wrong, and if you're wrong, I'm right.

Joey: But you still didn't convince me.

Nick: I'm not after you. I'm after them (*pointing to the public at large*).

★ CHAPTER 7 ★

Kick-Ass Arguments: A Step-by-Step Guide

If you've got them by the balls, their hearts and minds will follow.

—Anonymous

N ow that you're primed for battle, it's time to get down and dirty and argue the issues. Here you'll find shorthand guides to help you win arguments on a fistful of key issues at the core of today's left–right debate. We'll show you how to frame arguments to your advantage, hammer home compelling points, slap down your opponents' counterarguments, and bludgeon them with damning facts.

As a general rule—and to protect your own sanity—it's best to steer clear of radioactive issues like abortion, God, guns, and gays, which, let's face it, propel liberals into instant histrionics. That's not to say you can't make potent arguments on those issues; they're just not your best cards to play. You'll be better off going for the jugular on issues like taxes and terrorism, where you can have a more sober-minded debate.

While we can't guarantee victory in every case, we can show you how to keep your opponents on the defensive and upend their reality. You'll need to draw on your newly acquired skills to flesh out the details and deflect your opponents' specific attacks, but consider this a basic primer to steer you in the right direction.

CONSERVATISM: WHY IT PROMOTES INDIVIDUAL LIBERTY

STEP 1: FRAME YOUR ARGUMENT

Define conservative values as American values, from which this country has derived its strength and character. Contrast that to liberal values, from which this country has derived things like the welfare state and *Girls Gone Wild*.

STEP 2: MAKE YOUR CASE

* We have conservatism to thank for many of America's proudest achievements in the last quarter century, including winning the Cold War, reigning in the welfare state, bringing tax rates back to Earth, charting the course to defeat Islamic fascism, ridding the world of Saddam Hussein, and eradicating Oval Office fellatio.

* Conservatism stands for promoting core American values: a strong defense, free markets, lower taxes, limited government, personal responsibility, family values, and the

belief that all Americans have a right to life, liberty, and the pursuit of whatever they damn well please.

★ Conservatism stands against liberal values that divide us—penalizing hard work, waging class warfare, demonizing people of faith, undermining our troops, enforcing political correctness, and propagating the idea that no matter how lazy or stupid you are, everyone is a winner.

A conservative is a person who comes to Bentonville, Arkansas, to study Wal-Mart and learn how to fix the post office. A liberal is a person who comes to Bentonville, Arkansas, to make Wal-Mart like the post office.

—Newt Gingrich

STEP 3: REFUTE BOGUS CLAIMS

The "Conservatives-Are-Only-Out-for-Themselves" Defense

Kick-ass comeback: You say it like it's a bad thing. Our country was founded on the idea of promoting individual liberty. Conservatives believe everyone should have equal opportunity to make a buck and be happy—without being made to feel guilty about it. As for everyone else, conservatives believe the most compassionate thing we can do is to empower people to pull themselves up by their bootstraps. Liberals believe in handing out free boots, scolding you for putting them on wrong, and then charging you a boot tax.

The "Conservatives-Talk-a-Good-Game-but-Suck-at-Governing" Defense

Kick-ass comeback: For whatever failures conservatives have had in the past, they still did better than liberals would have done. The only time Republicans went wrong was when they lost sight of true conservative values like fiscal discipline and spending restraint. All Republicans have to do to make things right is to return to their core principles. Liberals have a bigger problem: they don't even know what their core principles are.

You will never hear a Republican say, 'Let's just cuddle and read the New Yorker tonight.' They understand you do not want reading materials in bed. You want a man.

—from *GQ* magazine's "The Elephant in the Bedroom: Ten (and a Half) Reasons Why Republicans—Yes, Republicans—Are the Best Party in Bed

The "Conservatives-Are-Against-Progress" Defense

Kick-ass comeback: If you define progress as raising taxes on American families, regulating the free market to death, infecting our children with Hollywood morality, and ensuring that every abortion-seeking illegal immigrant has a right to medicinal marijuana, then yes, conservatives are against progress, and proudly so.

STEP 4: BOTTOM-LINE IT

Whatever you may think about conservatives, you always know where they stand. And whether it's defending America or reigning in government, conservatives stand for doing what they believe is right, even if it's unpopular. Liberals, on the other hand, stand for doing what's expedient, usually after holding a finger to the wind. That's why, if we are looking for genuine leadership, we always will be better off with conservatives at the helm.

★ ★ ★ ★ ★ ★ ★ ★ ★ ★ ★ ★ ★ ★

Conservatism, by the Numbers

41: Percentage of Americans who identify themselves as conservative (2007 Gallup poll)

21: Percentage of Americans who identify themselves as liberal

47: Percentage of conservative Republicans who report to being "very happy" (2006 Pew poll)

28: Percentage of liberal Democrats who report to being "very happy"

1964: The last year in which a Democratic presidential candidate got more than 50.1 percent of the popular vote

20: Years out of the last twenty-eight in which Republicans have occupied the White House

Because you need me, Springfield. Your guilty conscience may force you to vote Democratic, but deep down you secretly long for a coldhearted Republican to lower taxes, brutalize criminals, and rule you like a king. That's why I did this: to protect you from yourselves. Now if you'll excuse me, I have a city to run.

—Sideshow Bob, on *The Simpsons*

TAXES AND THE ECONOMY: WHY CONSERVATISM IS BETTER FOR YOUR WALLET

STEP 1: FRAME YOUR ARGUMENT

Credit Republican tax cuts with the strong economic growth that followed the 2001 recession. Blame the budget deficit and runaway spending on the liberal tax-and-spenders in Congress who are busy greasing the wheels for the next recession.

STEP 2: MAKE YOUR CASE

★ Conservatives trust working Americans to spend their money more wisely than Nancy Pelosi can. When people have more cold cash in hand, it spurs investment, creates jobs, boosts the economy, and benefits everyone (with the possible exception of Al Sharpton, who is likely to remain unemployable in even the strongest economy).

★ Liberals believe any problem can be solved simply by throwing money at it. That's why they've never met a tax they didn't like: income, sales, property, automobile, alcohol, and gas taxes, you name it. If there were a way to tax the air you breathe, liberals would be on it quicker than Rosie O'Donnell on a puff pastry.

★ Republican economic policies under Reagan and Bush have created strong economic growth because conservatives believe the best thing government can do is get out of the way and let the free market work its Trumpesque magic.

STEP 3: REFUTE BOGUS CLAIMS

The "Republicans-Ran-Up-Huge-Deficits-and-Let-Spending-Run-Amok" Defense

Kick-ass comeback: Fighting a war is never cheap, and that's why Republicans were forced to increase spending when they controlled Congress. But now that Democrats are in power, where are the balanced budgets? Where is the spending restraint or the deficit reduction plan? If the Democrats want us to believe that they're fiscally responsible, why are they spending money like drunken Kennedys?

The "Republicans-Just-Want-to-Give-Tax-Cuts-to-the-Rich" Defense

Kick-ass comeback: It's a simple fact that the people who pay the most taxes are going to get the biggest tax cuts. The idea of taking people's hard-earned money and redistributing it to people who didn't earn it isn't fair and it's anti-American. In fact, it's called socialism.

The "Clinton-Balanced-the-Budget-and-Created-a-Booming-Economy" Defense

Kick-ass comeback: Yeah, and he did it thanks to a Republican Congress that prevented him from passing more tax increases and forced him to rein in spending. And let's not forget the fact that we were running deficits for a half century before that under control of a Democratic Congress. No one argues that the economy fared well when Clinton was in office. But after the bubble burst, he left us all stuck in a recession at the end of his term, clinging to our worthless Pets.com stock.

Republicans believe every day is the Fourth of July, but Democrats believe every day is April 15.

—Ronald Reagan

STEP 4: BOTTOM-LINE IT

Liberals are long on economic gripes but short on ideas. Tax hikes are not a recipe for balancing the budget, knee-jerk distrust of big business is not an economic plan, and more government regulation doesn't help entrepreneurs. The true conservative position is simple: let people keep more of their own money, cut wasteful Washington spending, and then sit back and let market forces fan us while feeding us grapes.

Any rich man does more for society than all the jerks pasting 'Visualize World Peace' bumper stickers on their cars. The worst leech of a merger and acquisitions lawyer making $500,000 a year will, even if he cheats on his taxes, put $100,000 into the public coffers. That's $100,000 worth of education, charity, or U.S. Marines. And the Marine Corps does more to promote world peace than all the Ben & Jerry's ice cream ever made.

—P. J. O'Rourke

★ ★ ★ ★ ★ ★ ★ ★ ★ ★ ★ ★ ★

The Economy, by the Numbers

2 million+: The average number of annual new jobs created since mid-2003, when Republican tax cuts fully kicked in

$2.4 trillion: Tax revenues in 2006, the highest in history

$2,500: The tax relief Republicans provided to 44 million American families with children in 2005

$2,000: The tax increase a family of four with an income of $50,000 would receive if Republicans' tax cuts expire

$31.6 trillion: The value of financial assets in America in 2001

$40 trillion: The value of financial assets in America in 2006

Didn't you wonder why you were getting checks for doing absolutely nothing?

—Bart Simpson

I figured 'cause the Democrats were in power again.

—Grandpa, on *The Simpsons*

DEFENDING AMERICA: WHY LIBERALS CAN'T HACK IT

STEP 1: FRAME YOUR ARGUMENT

Explain that if we want to kick serious ass and win the war on terror we need to take aggressive action and make our enemies quiver in their explosives-strapped vests. Self-deluding liberals, on the other hand, remain in such a state of denial that not even their therapists can talk them out of their pre-9/11 mindset.

STEP 2: MAKE YOUR CASE

★ The 9/11 attacks showed us that there are evil, maniacal people in the world who will destroy us the minute we let down our guard. We have to kill them before they kill us, and that means fighting them on the streets of Baghdad and Kabul so we don't have to fight them at the Olive Garden and Jamba Juice.

★ We have been at war with terrorists for decades, from the 1983 Beirut bombing to Al Qaeda strikes throughout the 1990s. We failed

to respond effectively while Clinton was busy
chubby chasing, but now the Bush administration has taken the fight directly to the enemy.

★ Liberals don't have the balls to fight the war
on terror. Most liberals will freely admit that
their own leaders aren't aggressive enough
when it comes to fighting for what they
believe. And that's exactly the kind of character flaw we can't afford when it comes to
waging war against a ruthless enemy.

Why not go to war just for oil? We need
oil. What do Hollywood celebrities imagine
fuels their private jets? How do they think
their cocaine is delivered to them?

—Ann Coulter

STEP 3: REFUTE BOGUS CLAIMS

The "Bush-Has-Failed-to-Go-After-the-Terrorists-Who-Attacked-Us" Defense

Kick-ass comeback: The fact is, we toppled the
Taliban in Afghanistan and we've either killed Al

Qaeda's top leaders or chased them into isolation and irrelevance. Whether or not you agree with the war in Iraq, we've sent a clear message to rogue nations and terrorists everywhere: Mess with us, and we'll blow you straight into the afterlife where you'll be surrounded by seventy-two *male* virgins who look like Kim Jong-il.

> Liberals are generous with other people's money, except when it comes to questions of national survival when they prefer to be generous with other people's freedom and security.
>
> —William F. Buckley Jr.

The "Republicans-Haven't-Done-Squat-to-Protect-the-Homeland" Defense

Kick-ass comeback: Republicans passed the Patriot Act, created the Department of Homeland Security, and deployed a nearly operational missile defense system. Republicans have also made it easier to conduct terrorist surveillance and Jack Bauer–style interrogations. What have liberals done? They've opposed most of those things while whining about violating the civil liberties of would-be terrorists. How does that make us safer?

The "Republicans-Have-Used-the-War-on-Terror-to-Divide-Us" Defense

Kick-ass comeback: If anyone has been divisive, it's liberals. If you were to ask most liberals who makes them angrier, Bush or the terrorists, most liberals would say Bush. Which raises the question, Wouldn't we all be better off if liberals spent more time fixating on Al Qaeda and the enemies of freedom and less time channeling Harry Belafonte and bashing Bush? Aren't we all supposed to be on the same side?

> Occasionally we're going to have to smoke one of these jagoffs into little sheikhlets to remind the world that we're not to be trifled with, and that while we have an incredibly long fuse, at the end of the day, it is connected to a big-ass bomb. We cannot afford to look soft in this dangerous world.
>
> —Dennis Miller

STEP 4: BOTTOM-LINE IT

Like it or not, we are involved in a long-term struggle against Islamic extremism. Conservatives understand the stakes and what it takes to win. With or without the help of liberals, conservatives intend to defeat the terrorists, just as we defeated Nazism, fascism, communism, imperial Japan, and hippies.

★ ★ ★ ★ ★ ★ ★ ★ ★ ★ ★ ★ ★

Defending America by the Numbers

7,000+: The number of Al Qaeda terrorists who have been killed since 9/11

8 years: The amount of time the Clinton administration had to get Osama bin Laden

8 months: The amount of time the Bush administration had to get bin Laden before 9/11

2 times: The increase in the number of border agents, as well as funding for border security, during Bush's presidency

6 million: The number of people attempting to enter the United States illegally who have been apprehended and sent home since Bush took office

0: The number of terror attacks on U.S. soil nearly six years after 9/11

IRAQ: WHY FAILURE IS NOT AN OPTION

STEP 1: FRAME YOUR ARGUMENT

Talk about the Iraq war in the context of 9/11 and the larger war on terror. Don't let liberals draw you into an argument about how we got into the war. Instead, focus on the need to continue helping Iraqis defend their country, and contrast that to following the beaten liberal path to surrender.

You cannot win a war if you tell the enemy you're going to quit.

—Dick Cheney

STEP 2: MAKE YOUR CASE

★ Like it or not, Iraq is a central part of the war against the terrorist bastards who are trying to destroy us. We learned from 9/11 that we need to take preemptive action against any potential threats. Iraq remains a threat, and the inconvenient truth liberals don't understand is that their asses are on the line too.

★ Withdrawing U.S. troops would likely drag Iran, Syria, and Saudi Arabia into a wider war, which would be like dropping a hornet's nest on a bonfire. And we're the ones who'd get stung where it hurts most.

★ We owe it to the Iraqi people to give them every chance to live in freedom. The best way to do that is to help stabilize the situation and train Iraqi forces to provide for their own long-term security. As the saying goes, give a man a fish, and you feed him for a day. But teach a man to fish out insurgents with an AK-47, and you help him save his country.

> If Saddam rejects peace and we have to use force, our purpose is clear. We want to seriously diminish the threat posed by Iraq's weapons of mass destruction program.
>
> —Bill Clinton, in 1998

STEP 3: REFUTE BOGUS CLAIMS

The "Republicans-Lied-about-the-Threat-Posed-by-Iraq" Defense

Kick-ass comeback: Bill Clinton, Hillary Clinton, John Kerry, and other leading Democrats all looked at the same intelligence over the last ten years and concluded that Saddam Hussein posed a threat. Were they lying too?

The "We-Already-Lost-the-War-So-Let's-Go-Home" Defense

Kick-ass comeback: Let's define what losing in Iraq would actually mean—U.S. troops retreating while terrorists overrun the country and turn it into another Afghanistan. It would also mean giving the Al Qaeda types free rein to acquire WMDs (like that nuclear bomb they've been eyeing in Kim Jong-il's window), and watching helplessly as they terrorize the entire world. How can we possibly throw in the towel now when those are the stakes?

The "We-Have-to-Set-a-Timetable-for-Withdrawal" Defense

Kick-ass comeback: So we're supposed to just tell the enemy how long we're planning to stay and hope that will make everyone less prone to attack? That's an exit strategy that might help extricate you from a dinner with the in-laws, but it's not a plan for victory in Iraq.

Is Iraq an optimum scenario? No, it isn't. Is it ever in war? Do I wish there was a country called "Al Qaedia" where we could have started all this? Of course I do, but guess what — there isn't. So Saddam Hussein and his punk sons were just unlucky enough to draw the Wonka ticket in the asshole lottery.

—Dennis Miller

STEP 4: BOTTOM-LINE IT

The best way to take a bad situation in Iraq and make it right is to do everything we can to help Iraqis help themselves. And that means not abandoning them in the middle of a fight—or stabbing our own troops in the back by cutting off their funding. If we surrender, as liberals want us to do, we'll do so much lasting damage to our standing in the world that future generations of Americans will wonder if we were French.

★ ★ ★ ★ ★★ ★ ★ ★ ★ ★ ★ ★ ★

Iraq, by the Numbers

26.7 million: The number of Iraqis now living in freedom

8 million: The number of Iraqis who voted in free and fair elections for the first time in 2005

1998: The year in which the Clinton administration made "regime change" the official government position on Iraq

$21 billion: Pork-barrel spending congressional Democrats packed into an emergency Iraq funding bill that included money for spinach growers, shrimp fisherman, and peanut storage

240,000: The number of Iraqi security forces that have been trained and equipped to protect their fellow citizens (as of 2006)

200 years and counting: The amount of time it has taken to get American democracy right

LIBERALISM: WHY IT'S WEAK AND WRONG

STEP 1: FRAME YOUR ARGUMENT

Portray liberalism as a misguided ideology of, by, and for elitist hypocrites who think they are morally superior because they recycle more than you and have adopted more African orphans. Whatever the issue at hand, point to nutty liberals and their ideological mushiness as the root cause of the problem.

STEP 2: MAKE YOUR CASE

★ Liberalism is an ideology based on the idea that 1. government can make wiser decisions than individuals; 2. people shouldn't be forced to accept personal responsibility; and 3. "anything goes" when it comes to morality, especially if it involves Astroglide.

★ Liberals love to extol their exemplary virtue, despite their own rampant hypocrisy. They rail against the evils of the same corporations in which they own shares. They say the earth is warming and the sky is falling, as they gas up their SUVs. And so on.

★ Liberals see the world in so many shades of gray that it pains them to take a simple stand on an issue. When they do, it's usually at a protest to save the whales, get out of Iraq, shut down the IMF, and impeach Bush. They want us to believe they can run the country, yet they can't even run a rally without confusing everyone.

STEP 3: REFUTE BOGUS CLAIMS

The "Liberals-Represent-the-Common-Man-and-Common-Good" Defense

Kick-ass comeback: Liberals say they're for the "little guy," but at bottom, they're elitists. They side with activist judges over the will of the people, put the demands of tree-hugging eco-wackos ahead of working Americans, and better identify with Ben Affleck than Joe Sixpack. If liberals are so committed to defending the "common man," why are they constantly telling him what he's doing wrong?

The "Liberals-Are-More-Tolerant-than-Conservatives" Defense

Kick-ass comeback: Let's see: If you oppose affirmative action, liberals will denounce you as a racist. If you believe in taking a strong stand against illegal immigration, you're a xenophobe. If you think marriage should be between a man and a woman, that's homophobic. Anyone who fails to support the liberal agenda gets tarred as bigoted, intolerant, or in the favorite liberal catchall for all of the above: fascist. How's that for tolerance?

"The 2006-Election-Was-a-Victory-for-Liberalism" Defense

Kick-ass comeback: Democrats won in 2006 because a handful of candidates in the red states played dress-up and ran as conservatives on issues like abortion and guns. No one got elected touting their liberal credentials, promising tax hikes, or marching under the banner of San Francisco values. If anything, the 2006 election was a confirmation that the country has moved further to the right.

They say Democrats don't stand for anything. That's patently untrue. We do stand for anything.

—Barack Obama

Liberal Nuttiness, by the Numbers

29,800: Google hits for "Bush is a Nazi"

16,300: Google hits for "Hitler was a Nazi"

26,000: Google hits for "Republicans are evil"

715: Google hits for "Satan is evil"

11,700: Google hits for "I hate conservatives"

808: Google hits for "I hate terrorists"

(from April 2007)

STEP 4: BOTTOM-LINE IT

It's been said that a liberal is someone who won't take his own side in an argument. The fact is, liberals find many of their own ideas so unconvincing that they spend most of their time bickering among themselves. That's not a governing philosophy. That's an episode of *The View*. Bill Clinton once advised liberals that in times of crisis it is better to be strong and wrong than weak and right. But liberals still don't get it. Their problem is that they are weak *and* wrong.

No one is fond of taking responsibility for his actions, but consider how much you'd have to hate free will to come up with a political platform that advocates killing unborn babies but not convicted murderers. A callous pragmatist might favor abortion and capital punishment. A devout Christian would sanction neither. But it takes years of therapy to arrive at the liberal point of view.

—P. J. O'Rourke

It isn't that liberals are ignorant. It's just that they know so much that isn't so.

—Ronald Reagan

CHAPTER 8

The Liberal Hall of Shame

I have only ever made one prayer to God, a very short one: 'Oh Lord, make my enemies ridiculous.' And God granted it.

—Voltaire

You can add extra bite to your arguments by highlighting outstanding achievements in liberal hypocrisy and idiocy. Happily, there are many fine examples from which to choose.

Here's a rundown of some of the most prominent liberal sex fiends, morons, crooks, and celebrity blowhards who have disgraced national politics in recent years—and earned their place in the Liberal Hall of Shame.

THE WING OF SEX FIENDS, PERVERTS, AND ADULTERERS

BILL "I FEEL YOUR SOMETHING-OR-OTHER" CLINTON

Claim to shame: A thong. A cigar. A stained dress. A finger-wagging denial. An independent counsel report that read like *Penthouse*'s letters to the editor. A new definition for "is." Needless to say, the Clinton-Lewinsky affair will forever remain the sex scandal by which all future Washington sex scandals will be judged. It takes special talent to degrade your office and your marriage in that kind of spectacular fashion. As Dennis Miller put it, "If Bill Clinton were any more low rent, he'd be a spring break destination."

JIM MCGREEVEY, TRUCKER TEMPTRESS

Claim to shame: The former New Jersey governor resigned after confessing to carrying on a secret homosexual affair with an Israeli poet. Later, in a tell-all book, McGreevey also recounted how he used to cruise highway rest stops to have anonymous sex with gay truckers. Jay Leno asked the pertinent question: "At what point do you stop having anonymous sex at truck stops and say to yourself, 'I'm tired of this, I'd rather be governor'?"

JESSE "WHO'S YOUR DADDY" JACKSON

Claim to shame: He may have never held a real job, but Reverend Jackson has long held himself up as the personification of liberal moral superiority. This is why it was especially rich when he fathered a child out of wedlock. Better still, he knocked up his mistress while he was ministering to Bill Clinton during the Monica Lewinsky affair. The scandal gave "clearer meaning to the Rainbow Coalition's Operation 'Push,'" quipped Jon Stewart.

TED KENNEDY, WORLD'S WORST DATE

Claim to shame: Say what you will about all the other adulterers and sex fiends in Washington, but no one else ever drove their date off a bridge, left her to drown, and then fled the scene of the crime. Years later, the irony was apparently lost on Kennedy when he decided to name his dog "Splash," which is sort of like Bill Clinton naming a dog "BJ."

BARNEY FRANK, PARAGON OF MASSACHUSETTS VALUES

Claim to shame: The openly gay Massachusetts congressman hired a gay prostitute he met through a personals ad as a staff member in the 1980s. Frank was reprimanded by the House in 1990 amid revelations that the man was running a prostitution ring out of Frank's apartment. Apparently those are the kinds of values Massachusetts liberals expect their representatives to champion, judging from the 66 percent margin by which they reelected Frank that year.

THE WING OF MORONS

DAN "CRAZIER THAN A SQUIRREL IN A CAGE" RATHER

Claim to shame: When he wasn't breathlessly reporting on forged National Guard memos, the former CBS anchor regularly demonstrated that he was both literally and metaphorically insane. To borrow a few Ratherisms, his credibility was as thin as turnip soup, his brand of journalism would give an aspirin a headache, he got beaten in the ratings like a rented mule, and his legacy remains shakier than cafeteria Jell-O. Nevertheless, Rather continues to insist his grasp of reality is spandex-tight.

JOHN "FLIP-FLOP" KERRY

Claim to shame: It wasn't enough to lose one presidential election. Just when he was gearing up for another run, Kerry said, "You know, education—if you make the most of it—you study hard, you do your homework, and you make an effort to be smart, you can do well. If you don't, you get stuck in Iraq." Kerry insisted it was a botched joke aimed at President Bush, not the troops. But as Dick Cheney quipped, "I guess we didn't get the nuance. He was for the joke before he was against it."

HOWARD "THE SCREAM" DEAN

Claim to shame: The Democratic Party chairman may be best known for his infamous scream, but that's hardly the most objectionable thing to come out of his mouth. He has called the GOP "evil," "corrupt," and "brain-dead," labeled the GOP a "white Christian party" with a lot of people who "have never made an honest living in their lives," and flatly stated that he "hates Republicans and everything they stand for." And he accuses *Republicans* of being divisive.

CYNTHIA "SUCKER PUNCH" MCKINNEY

Claim to shame: Perhaps the loosest canon in the entire Democratic arsenal, former Congresswoman McKinney (D-Unemployed) punched a Capitol Hill police officer in the chest when she refused to stop at a security checkpoint. Naturally, she played the race card, accusing the officer of racial profiling. Her lawyer said she was guilty of "being in

Congress while black." Now she is out of Congress due to being insane.

RAY "CHOCOLATE CITY" NAGIN

Claim to shame: The New Orleans mayor failed to dispatch the city's buses to evacuate residents prior to Hurricane Katrina. Later, he failed to dispatch his brain when he proclaimed, "I don't care what people are saying Uptown or wherever they are. This city will be chocolate at the end of the day." As Amy Poehler joked, "And he will be the delicious nut in the center."

"CHILLARY" CLINTON

Claim to shame: For anyone who may have wondered if we all would have been better off had Hillary stayed home baking cookies, consider the following words of wisdom by the lesser Clinton: "We're going to take things away from you on behalf of the common good," "I'm not going to have some reporters pawing through our papers. We are the president," "God bless the America we're trying to create." God bless it indeed.

CINDY "LONGEST FIFTEEN MINUTES EVER" SHEEHAN

Claim to shame: Has there ever been a more confused peace activist with a louder megaphone in the history of America? Consider the following remarks by Cindy Sheehan: "(George Bush) is ten times the terrorist that Osama ever was," "This country is not worth dying for," "You get America out of Iraq and Israel out of Palestine, and you'll stop the terrorism," "We are waging a nuclear war in Iraq right now. That country is contaminated. It will be contaminated for practically eternity now." She makes Jane Fonda look like a seasoned diplomat.

THE WING OF CROOKS AND DEGENERATES

JAMES "BEAM ME UP" TRAFICANT

Claim to shame: Arguably the nuttiest congressman of all time, Traficant used to end his colorful floor speeches by saying "beam me up"—until he was thrown in jail for bribery, racketeering, and tax fraud. He also forced his staff to clean horse stalls on his farm and work on his house-boat. Asked by the House Ethics Committee to explain his need for a houseboat, the Democratic gadfly said, "I wanted to have Playboy bunnies come on at night to meet with me. I wanted to be promiscuous with them." He also said when he gets out of jail, he will "grab a sword like Maximus Meridius Demidius, and as a gladiator I will stab people in the crotch."

PATRICK KENNEDY, UNSAFE AT ANY SPEED

Claim to shame: Proving once again why you should never mix Kennedys with alcohol, Ted Kennedy's son, Patrick, plowed his car into a U.S. Capitol barrier at 3:00 a.m. one night after a drunken bender. He claimed to a police officer that he was on his way to vote. But as Bill Maher joked, Kennedy really didn't "remember anything about the accident, except a huge sense of relief when he came to and he wasn't soaking wet."

WILLIAM "COLD CASH" JEFFERSON

Claim to shame: Only in Washington can you find someone who even maintains his innocence after being caught on video accepting a bribe and hiding $90,000 in cash in the freezer. And only in Louisiana can you win reelection for that sort of thing, as Congressman Jefferson did while awaiting indictment.

SANDY BERGER, THE POOR MAN'S INDIANA JONES

Claim to shame: Before testifying to the 9/11 commission, Sandy Berger, Clinton's national security adviser, embarked on a quest to retrieve highly classified documents at the National Archives. Hoping to elude archive officials, he reportedly stuffed several documents into his socks and exited the building. According to his guilty plea, once outside, he hid the documents under a construction trailer. Later, he spirited the documents back to his office, where he cut them up with scissors. When archive officials confronted him about the missing documents, he then went on a desperate hunt to find the trash collector, to no avail. This from the guy in charge of protecting America during the Clinton administration.

The Wing of Celebrity Blowhards

Match the following crazed liberal celebrities with their idiotic statements below.

1. Michael Moore
2. Sean Penn
3. Rosie O'Donnell
4. Cameron Diaz
5. Harry Belafonte
6. Linda Ronstadt
7. Kanye West
8. Margaret Cho

a. "George Bush is not Hitler. He would be if he fucking applied himself."

b. "The Iraqis who have risen up against the occupation are not 'insurgents' or 'terrorists' or 'The Enemy.' They are the REVOLUTION, the Minutemen, and their numbers will grow—and they will win."

c. "We have a voice now, and we're not using it, and women have so much to lose. I mean, we could lose the right to our bodies... If you think that rape should be legal, then don't vote."

d. "No matter what the greatest tyrant in the world, the greatest terrorist in the world, George W. Bush says, we're here to tell you: Not hundreds, not thousands, but millions of the American people...support your revolution."—speaking alongside Venezuelan President Hugo Chavez

e. "I think that people like the Howard Sterns, the Bill O'Reillys, and to a lesser degree the bin Ladens of the world are making a horrible contribution."

f. "I worry that some people are entertained by the idea of this war. They don't know anything about the Iraqis, but they're angry and frustrated in their own lives. It's like Germany before Hitler took over. The economy was bad and people felt kicked around. They looked for a scapegoat. Now we've got a new bunch of Hitlers."

g. "George Bush doesn't care about black people... They're giving the Army permission to go down and shoot us." —on the government's response to Hurricane Katrina in New Orleans

h. "Don't fear the terrorists. They're mothers and fathers."

Answers: 1. b, 2. e, 3. h, 4. c. 5. d, 6. f, 7. g, 8. a

★ **CHAPTER 9** ★

You've Won the Battle, Now Help Win the War

We gotta take these bastards. Now we could do it with conventional weapons. But that could take years and cost millions of lives. No, I think we have to go all-out. I think that this situation absolutely requires a really futile and stupid gesture be done on somebody's part.

—from *Animal House*

Now that you've succeeded in tearing apart, taunting, or humiliating your opponents, you can set your sights on loftier goals—helping to defeat liberalism at large. There are, of course, the conventional things you should do as a matter of habit: vote, get others to vote, contribute money to campaigns and causes, and get educated (for a list of essential political resources, news sites, and blogs, see FightLiberals.com).

But if you want to make a serious ruckus, you need to step up your game. With that in mind, we offer . . .

SIX UNCONVENTIONAL THINGS YOU CAN DO TO SAVE THE WORLD FROM LIBERALS

1. MAKE CONSERVATIVE BABIES

There's good news for the long-term conservative effort to win new recruits. According to the 2004 General Social Survey, conservatives are reproducing at a rate that is 41 percent higher than liberals. It's imperative that conservatives help keep the trend going.

What you need: A conservative of opposite gender, mood music

What you do: We don't really need to spell it out here, but let's just say it's time for conservatives to get busy and start popping out new foot soldiers or, if you prefer, adopting them. For those still looking for that special someone, you can do your part to multiply the conservative ranks by going to ConservativeMatch.com or RepublicanPassions.com today.

2. STALK A DEMOCRATIC CANDIDATE

Sure, you can write your congressman. But if you really want to make an impact, follow him around with a video camera. There's a Democratic candidate out there just waiting to self-immolate, and it's your job to provide the match.

What you need: Video camera, campaign schedule, YouTube account

What you do: By becoming a fixture at public events, you will be in a unique position to record any idiotic utterances that may sink his career.

That's what S. R. Sidarth did when he followed around former Republican Senator George Allen. When Allen ridiculed the twenty-year-old American of Indian descent by calling him "macaca" (a term for monkeys used as an ethnic slur in certain parts of the world), the video ended up on YouTube and sent Allen's campaign into a tailspin, ultimately costing the Republicans the Senate. The challenge now falls to conservatives to pay back Democrats in kind.

3. STAGE A CLEVER PROTEST

If you really want to advance your political interests while making a name for yourself, you need to do something that will grab headlines.

What you need: A vivid imagination, a sense of irony, a lawyer

What you do: Pick a topical issue and put your own spin on it. One of the more imaginative protests staged in recent years came in response to the Supreme Court's unanimous (and universally unpopular) decision allowing the government to seize land belonging to private citizens under eminent domain law. In response, Logan Darrow

Clements of Los Angeles launched a campaign to encourage the city of Weare, New Hampshire, to seize Justice David Souter's home and turn it into the "Lost Liberty Hotel," arguing that a luxury hotel would better serve the community. The effort failed, but not before Clements made headlines and drew attention to the utter absurdity of the ruling.

4. BECOME A MOLE

You can help the conservative cause by infiltrating the ranks of the liberal opposition and working to destroy them from the inside.

What you need: A good poker face and a resistance to Kool-Aid

What you do: Get a job working on a Democratic campaign, then leak information to Republican operatives or reporters, write an anonymous blog, or prepare a tell-all book. Join the ranks of MoveOn.org, the ACLU, or Al Franken's joke-writing staff, win their trust, and then start parceling out extremely bad advice. Or land a gig as a left-wing pundit, string everyone along for a few years, and then right before the election denounce the Democratic candidate live on CNN and openly pledge allegiance to the GOP.

5. EXORCISE LIBERAL MEDIA BIAS

Combating liberal media bias requires more than simply turning to FOX News, conservative talk radio, and right-wing blogs. It requires taking the fight directly to the enemy.

What you need: TV, radio, Internet access, and an axe to grind

What you do: Forget letters to the editor. Write directly to the reporter or to his or her editor or producer to complain about a biased story. That's how you can get inside their heads. In more egregious cases—say, if CBS News is peddling forged memos about Bush's National Guard service—make noise at the corporate level, boycott advertisers, or write investor relations and tell them you're selling off your shares (even if you don't own any). Your goal is to use every tool available to beat objectivity into the media beast.

6. HAUNT DEMOCRATS FROM THE GRAVE

If you can figure out a way to vote while dead, as many decomposing Chicagoans have over the years, great. But if you want to make a truly memorable political statement, try your obituary.

What you need: To be dead

What you do: Ask your loved ones to honor your memory the way the family of James E. Fete Sr. of Ohio did: "In lieu of flowers, vote Bush."

After-*Words*

If you can't answer a man's argument, all is not lost; you can still call him vile names.

—Elbert Hubbard

WHEN ALL ELSE FAILS: 27,000 WAYS TO INSULT LIBERALS

Can't persuade anyone to your way of thinking? Kill 'em with words instead. This handy chart contains 27,000 potential insults you can lob at liberals. Choose a word from each column, string them together, and fire away at all the "spineless, sushi-eating weasels," or "godless, liberal media–parroting defeatocrats" in your midst.

Column A	Column B	Column C
spineless	America-blaming	defeatocrats
godless	Hollywood-humping	elitists
morally superior	Bible-bashing	pagans
angry	Jesus-trashing	sinners
knee-jerk	tax-hiking	socialists
irrational	terrorist-coddling	appeasers
hysterical	gun-grabbing	moonbats
unmedicated	stem cell–sucking	crybabies
obnoxious	race card–playing	whiners
pathetic	criminal-pampering	wusses
out-of-touch	culture war–waging	extremists
amoral	abortion-promoting	demoncrats
confused	morality-destroying	sodomites
bedwetting	French-fellating	surrender monkeys
loony	liberal media–parroting	pantywaists
naïve	cut-and-running	flip-floppers
unpatriotic	troop-slandering	girlie men
unhinged	flag-burning	hippies
deranged	body-piercing	potheads
politically correct	vegan-exalting	tree huggers
weak	welfare-glorifying	softies
sanctimonious	victim-playing	hypocrites
brainless	business-bashing	bleeding hearts
out-of-control	values-perverting	sex fiends

Column A	Column B	Column C
anti-American	ACLU-revering	snobs
lying	trial lawyer–deifying	flakes
militant	MoveOn.org-genuflecting	demagogues
wasteful	class war–fomenting	weasels
reckless	sushi-eating	losers
dangerous	Satan-appeasing	douche bags

Acknowledgments

This book would not have been necessary if it hadn't been for the politicians on both sides who have worked so diligently to divide the country. Nor would it have been possible—or at least not as much fun to write—without the inspiration provided by Jon Stewart, Stephen Colbert, Bill Maher, Dennis Miller, and political humorists everywhere who put politics in perspective and help dull the pain.

I am indebted to my editor, Deb Werksman; her assistant, Susie Benton; and the staff at Sourcebooks, whose hard work and enthusiasm made this book a reality; and to my agent, Barret Neville, whose editorial guidance and vision helped shape this project.

Many thanks to Thomas Fahy, who offered indispensable feedback, careful editing, and unflagging support from the beginning, and to Todd Smithline, Lou Kipilman, Joshua Swartz, Lee Levine, Max Zarzana, Josh Archibald, Daniel

Wasson, and Sarah Schroeder—all of whom provided valuable assistance and shrewd insights (as well as a few good punch lines) during many stages of the writing process. I'd also like to give a special shout-out to John Thong Nein for challenging me to a war of wits (the shoe is now on the other foot).

My family provided not only inspiration but, somewhat inadvertently, much of the field research that helped inform this book. I am grateful for the love and support of my parents, Ken and Caryl, who taught me the value of tolerance and spirited debate, and my brother, Todd, who taught me the importance of defending my position, especially while being hunted with a BB gun. To the DeCastros, a special salute to Mike for embracing his designation as "Uncle Blowhard" with a passion, Lois her creative inspiration, and Baylee for living the radical liberal dream. To Jessica Garrett, Patty, Neil, and the entire Smithline clan, thank you for your loving encouragement and the lively conversations, and for demonstrating the importance of communicating in crisp sound bites.

I am also endlessly grateful to many friends for their unfailing support: David Ziring, Alison

Hickey, Shannon Farley, Danielle Svetcov, Alex Kazan, Aviva Rosenthal, Liana Schwarz, Jodi and Andy Brown, Lesley Reidy, Kim O'Farrell, Marty Chester, Dave Uram, Mitch Cox, Rebecca Bagdadi, Jeremy and Melody Hannebrink-Vance, Carol Brydolf, the Suffin family, and the numerous other family members and friends who took time to share their political wisdom and partisan horror stories.

I'd also like to acknowledge several important influences that shaped my political and humor sensibilities: Matt Dorf, my former bureau chief, who schooled me in the ways of Washington; Donal Brown, my high school journalism teacher, who showed me how to kill 'em with words; Dave Kreines, a master of both words and wit, and one of the best friends I ever knew; and the late Duane Garrett, one of the funniest commentators and most brilliant political minds of his generation.

And most importantly, I am grateful beyond words to my wife, Laura, who inspires me every day. Her abiding faith, brilliant insights, and sharp editing helped make every part of this book better. Her love and laughter make every part of life better, too.

About the Author

Daniel Kurtzman chronicles the absurdities of politics as editor of politicalhumor.about.com, the popular website that is part of The New York Times Company's About.com network. As a former Washington correspondent-turned-political satirist, his work has appeared in the *San Francisco Chronicle*, Salon.com, JTA, and the *Funny Times*, among other publications. He lives with his wife, Laura, in the San Francisco Bay Area, where he enjoys engaging in political squabbles with "red" and "blue" people alike. As an equal opportunity offender, Kurtzman is also the author of *How to Win a Fight with a Conservative*.